Sing Peace to Cedar River

Books by William M. Clark

TALES OF CEDAR RIVER
MORE TALES OF CEDAR RIVER
MAINE IS IN MY HEART
FROM THOUGHT TO THEME
THE BEST OF BILL CLARK
DOWN EAST HUMOR
SING PEACE TO CEDAR RIVER

SING PEACE TO CEDAR RIVER

by

William M. Clark

Drawings by Michael Ricci

Guy Gannett Publishing Co.
Portland/Maine

Published by Guy Gannett Publishing Co., 390 Congress Street, Portland, Maine 04101, September, 1982.

First edition printed in the United States of America by Gannett Graphics, Augusta, Maine 04330, September, 1982.

Library of Congress Catalog Card # 82-80953

ISBN # 0-930096-41-X

There can be no question on the dedication of this book, the final attempt to portray the Cedar River that was and is multiplied in all the Cedar Rivers of rurality. The book must be dedicated to all the women of the farming and logging communities whose young dreams of romance were uncomplainingly adjusted to reality but in whose eyes still glowed the knowledge of beauty denied to men.

In the lives of these women there were moments when wondrous things could have happened but, somehow, did not. Their need for beauty glowed but there were ripe berries to be canned. The need stormed at their minds but there were babies and kitchen gardens and dirty shirts and caulk marked floors to scrub and sometimes wood to carry and always loyalty to be displayed in spite of disillusionment.

In rurality, the creation of a matriarchy was never voluntary but rather forced. The solid saving strength was in the women. They held hard to a semblance of the gentility that kept discouraged semi-savagery from ruling.

This book is written by a man. For thousands of years men have covered their own confusion by pretending to scorn the guidance of the sane sex of the human species. In reality, the wisdom is welcomed but to save face it must be pictured as being amusing.

Forgive us our sins.

From here, look down.
There's Cedar River in that patch of mist.
Mist is a town product.
They make it down there and blame it on God.
They're lost in it and they'd be lost without it.
It brings peace.

The mist hides battles, stubbornness, worn out codes.
The mist makes harshness soft.
A man can weave it into songs.
Sing mist, sing softness, sing love;
Sing peace to Cedar River.

—Jonas P. Hall

Introduction

It was the season of uncertainties in Cedar River, the time when the sun's struggling circle barely cleared the ridgeline at full noon.

It was an interval of realism, a spasm of acceptance. There were no prayers for winter warmth. We knew that winter was already planned. The wind would bring what cold it willed. The skies would allocate what misery seemed due.

All this, hated but acknowledged, cursed but accepted, damned but not defied, was part of the heritage of every man in town, so nobody shook his fist at the hills when he noted the afternoon symptoms of coming snow.

Snow in itself was normality. There were folks who thought that a storm of unusual severity indicated divine displeasure with the town, but their opinions had no practical value, since, when the storm showed, it was too late to reform, too late to repent, too late to do anything except set a shovel handy to the door.

On this day, the signs were plain.

There was early darkness; earlier than normal; too early to induce comfort; very early.

Cedar River, centered in the intervales along the stream that shares its name, is guarded much too closely by the ridges and the foothills into which it sprawls, to be granted lengthy brightness on the best of winter days. When the clouds are solid, evening starts at noon.

That means a storm, unavoidable, probably deserved.

So, when darkness took possession of the clearing quickly, after this day which had been only a prolonged false dawn with no sun showing through the grayness, we expected snow, and snow came, quietly, with the night.

The flakes fell in solid succession, each fitting into its own shaped niche and keeping, thus, the blanket smooth as it was spread over contours of land and odd debris.

The smoke stayed low across the town. The beaten paths formed replicas of finger sweeps along a freshly plastered wall. The hillside springs grew blacker as their edges shaped themselves in new and untracked frames.

Ten hours it snowed.

Cedar River slept, its night lights showing as an earth-bound clustering of fifty-odd dim stars with here and there a flick of brightness, on and off, as fretful child was tended or someone rose to check a fire.

In the morning, the snow had stopped falling and the valley was silent. The ugly stains that marked activity from previous storms were gone. For a time too brief to measure, Cedar River was pristine.

The sun brought sounds. Tractors dominated small circles. Men's shouts crossed the fields and died against the barrier of woods. Shovels scraped, trace chains jangled, blades thudded as they backed and dropped.

Each working group was an island and the scattered noises were kept from blending by the muffling white mass.

Andy Caruthers and I met in our sawmill yard. We nodded to each other and then looked around at the picture book scene, concentrating as though viewing it in company were different, somehow, from our earlier unshared observations made when we had tidied up our own home areas and walked, alone, toward what we knew would be a mutual fatigue.

The sun was glinting from the trees by then, sparkling when it touched an icicle to which the filter of snow powder hadn't clung.

"A poet would call that beautiful," I said.

"We're shy on poets, thank God," said Andy. "Unless you're counting Jonas Hall."

"Why can't I?"

"No reason. It's your tally sheet. But he don't believe that snow is beautiful. He made that plain once, remember? But he ain't plain very often. In my book, he's a nut."

I didn't answer. Jonas Hall had puzzled people for so long that finally they settled things by saying he was simple minded. He was a double-action poet and that made the members of the Ladies' Literary Guild just as upset as it did the men in Turner's store on Saturday nights.

Jonas wrote earthy doggerel that delighted the rebels against piety. Then he angered the men he had just pleased by writing esoteric commentaries that might have won him admiration from the literary ladies had they not been in such a rage over the poems that had previously pleased the men.

The poem that Andy Caruthers spoke about... the snow poem... was put on paper because Jonas objected to the phrases of a lecturer who was hired by the Literary Guild to bring a package of culture to the town.

The lecturer was flabby, pasty-faced and porridge gutted. When he quoted from the Victorian poets, he closed his eyes as though he had a cue sheet on the inside of the lids. He had mastered a wondrous collection of cliches. He ran through the routine of "winter wonderland—mother nature-ice bedecked-sparkling snowflakes-frosted boughs-cathedral pines."

Jonas listened to about half the lecture and then he made a loud protest about the pain inflicted. He spoke one terse word which was a cry and a condemnation and a suggestion that he was not being filled with culture at all but rather with something else.

He might have gone on to more specific complaints but he

was understandably ejected from the hall so he went home and wrote a counterclaim which was remembered long after the lecturer was forgotten.

"They call them picturesque, you know,
Those wondrous woods, bough bent with snow.
But with that thought I don't agree,
For when, beneath a snow-draped tree,
I lift my head to view its grace,
I get the drapings in my face."

Men like Andy Caruthers approved of those sentiments. On that morning in the mill yard after the storm, so did I.

Because a snowstorm is a different thing to a man who can walk its whiteness until he is cold and then go back inside than it is to a worker who must stomp his feet and keep plugging.

We had to stomp and plug that morning.

We plowed the fresh fall from the packed base, adding the new surplus to the deposited old, narrowing our area of activity. We swept the snow from the lumber piles, fearing the temperature change that would glue each board to the sticker until spring.

We swept the headers, too, because it is easier to sweep than to pry until your guts grip your backbone, and there would be prying enough in spite of the sweeping.

In the afternoon, the wind came up. The air tightened. By the time we started for home, we could hear the forming crispness in the fields. We could sense the difference underfoot.

We knew it would be a cold night, a night when a wise man sat up later than usual, tending his fires so that their banking period would be briefer and the house warmer in the morning.

Andy's farewell at our place of parting was along that line of thought. "Keep stoking tonight, boy," he said. "Don't let the smoke freeze."

I could hear his heels squeak on the packed snow for awhile

and then the distance grew too great and I walked to the rhythm I set myself. I found myself picking up the thread of my musings about Jonas Hall. I theorized that Jonas' big problem was that he was constantly fighting against telling the truth.

The truth could be destructive to both memories and hopes, if it came through plainly enough to spread the understanding that when a man lives in Cedar River he doesn't live in any actual place. He lives in his own version of places undefined. He lives in mist, too, mostly, because what sun the hills let through is filtered by thick saplings and by twisted fence-line pines, and sometimes, by desire.

Cedar River is its own past and the past of many places, holding, for those places, things that they have lost or thrown away or never had, but thought they had.

It is Christian only by the presence of the church. By instinct, it is pagan.

Its history, in approximation, is no challenge to recite. Clint Reynolds, the Postmaster, can give a fairly full narration. So can Mr. Turner at the store, or even Randy Gage, father of too many children, who, in turn, begat too many of their own.

These men would add imaginative details to their history, but all would stay in reaching range of truth. There's no great secret about why the town was built. It grew because there had to be a place for men to find when they had fought their way upriver and through passes to the pockets in the ridges.

There was only one requirement for migration into Cedar River. Those who came had to believe in the existence of the town and of themselves.

They found a sometimes undesirable requirement for staying. They had to work. They plowed the intervales and tried to tame the ridges. They burned hardwood and sold the ashes. They barred out rocks and hauled them to the edges of the fields to build some mightly walls.

For their efforts, nature presented them with more rocks for more walls. They had walls in plenty.

They had clean water, too, and face-freshening mists. They

had timber. Timber became a part of their being, accepted and absorbed and transmitted to their sons.

They were surrounded by the forests that needed strength for the felling. Past them flowed the river. Down the river, year on year, the logs were carried, jamming, churning, taking toll of blood and broken bones.

This was the time of glory. This was power and shouting strength and challenge.

This was the eventual barricade to growth. An age that subsidizes softness drives few men to regions where hard work is habit.

That's the story. In its aftermath, the poorer farms were left to grow again to woods. The town retreated toward its center, accepting the fact of smallness, coming to like the semi-lethargy that allowed for idleness between the times of needed labor.

All families became old families.

Of necessity came voluntary trade restraint. The sawmill number is now stabilized. Old man Turner runs the only store that's needed, contemplated competition being recognized as folly that would draw for customers only those who wouldn't pay their bills.

Doc Yates conducts a medical monopoly, dispensing pills and fatherly advice, the former accepted suspiciously and the latter tucked away in mental crevices to be considered when its recipient feels better.

There's just one church. No one is positive about its doctrinal denomination, but it fights the Devil, not in mystic concept but physically, blow by blow. Every Sunday, Reverend Adams stands and challenges Satan to come out and fight.

Satan rarely does. He'd rather sneak around seducing folks. He finds that safer.

The Cedar River school still forces education down the throats of the reluctant young, even though Mrs. Kelly has retired after years of dedicated walloping and hearty slaps, motivations without fancy names but with the guarantee of proved success.

The facts of Cedar River life don't need interpretation on

the surface. It's when the stream goes underground that error becomes routine and truth puts on a costume that would seem more suitable for falsehood.

The local legal code, developed and refined, protects the residents from almost nothing but themselves, and that but rarely.

My Uncle Oscar manufactures blissful brews in tubs and crocks. He hides his operations from his thirsty neighbors rather than from Jesse Hill, policeman by election.

Complications that involve the sexes, married or unmarried, friends or enemies, involved or casual by-passers, backdoor romances or over-ardent viewing of the moon, all are settled somehow in a battle or a compromise or sometimes in a change from Mrs. This to Mrs. That.

Either way, the frowns are temporary. Ultimate acceptance is assured. There aren't enough folks in Cedar River to permit the luxury of social ostracism.

Judging sins in Cedar River must have practicality for guidance. When people cleanse their souls, at revival meeting time, a panic would set in if some stupid man confessed a violation of the game laws, thus embarrassing the pillars of the church who on their consciences had acts in kinship.

Surely no one would have been unkind enough to have thus shamed Minnie Trembley, who, before she died at Bennett Brook and forced the men to skid her from the gulley with a horse, had been foremost at shouting praises of the Lord and publicly upbraiding youngsters caught emerging from the fringe brush on warm summer evenings.

Would anyone have wanted Minnie to come forward to the sinners' bench and shout, "I have sinned . . . I ate six pounds of deer meat, September killed, for supper?"

What would have been accomplished by that?

Jonas Hall answered the question for me when I snarled myself in its specifics and its niceties.

"Accomplished?" he asked. "I'll tell you what it would have accomplished. It would have resulted in an empty hall when the next sin-confessing session was held. Then where would anybody get anything to talk about except what was guessed?"

There was always, and still is, one more great need in understanding Cedar River, alone and in the company of all the inland towns which make it one of many rather than unique. These small settlements have no continuity of purpose or of time. Their history is episodic.

That is what fools the social engineers, the planners, the bureaucrats, and the reformers. It fools the academics who want to analyze, to study the sequence of causes and effects.

In the Cedar Rivers, the planners are pathetic. They want to say, "At first, there was this, then there was that, and now, if we are to change this town and make it like the one we left because we did not like it, we must have a control board, a business board, a zoning board, an ethics board, and a social realignment board."

Unhappily, after spending $100,000, torn from the pockets of the screaming taxpayers, the planners find that no one wants to be realigned, zoned, or controlled. Neither does anyone remember when or why this changed to that.

But the same confusion faces the narrator. About that, too, I talked with Jonas Hall.

"A man trying to give a picture of a town should have a tidy sequence. He should have the history and show the progress."

"Garbage," said Jonas. "What history? What progress? You're thinking of that old bilge about there being a novel in the life of every man. Up here, there isn't. Nobody can keep his mind on anything except perhaps unusually dedicated adultry for long enough to make even a short story. You listen in the store. What gets talked about?"

"Personal adventure, mostly."

"Yeah. One each, maybe two. Over and over. Highlights, not continuity. A time the man was a hero. He can't go forward or back because he'd have to admit that those times he was a boob or a bum."

"The story has to be in segments, then?"

"Absolutely," said Jonas. "Segments viewed in dimness, with the beginning the same as the end. Doc Yates helping folks get born. Frustration making most of them wish Doc hadn't bothered. Poor Doc. St. Paul competing with a midway barker. Start with him. Then if you want some history, either admit it's all distorted or else spend ten years trying to separate what's true from what's imagined."

"Truth is unpopular. If you want a book on small towns to sell, you have to stress romance."

"Stress it, then, " said Jonas, " and leave the truth to me."

Some years, when old Doc Yates
Had managed to accumulate an extra dollar,
He'd go downriver to the medical convention.

He'd sit and listen to specifics of diseases
That he didn't dare to diagnose
For fear the town would hang him, sensing shame.

He'd see some fancy gadgets
That he never could afford to buy.
Then, for absolute fulfillment of frustration,
Some fat quack, who specialized
In holding hands with rich old ladies,
Always asked Doc how it felt
To have no competition in the curing business.
Doc had too much loyalty to Cedar River
To ask the question that he should have asked:

"How would you feel, you pompous jackass,
If your people never called you on a case
Until they'd almost killed the patient
By stuffing him with diced and stewed sheep droppings?"
Doc used to go to bed at night
Cursing the folkcure competition;
Saying, "Damn that Nanny-Plum Tea."

—Jonas P. Hall

Chapter I

Old Doc Yates carried pills in his satchel and sympathy for mankind in his heart. He was as much of a realist as he could be in a town that lived on the quivering edge of fantasy. He accepted the conflicts he faced.

Doc was philosophical about Cedar River practices in the face of injuries or diseases. He knew that most of the residents put more trust in herbs and mustard plasters than they did in the drugs he dispensed. He was resigned to his inability to break the local belief in horse chestnuts as rheumatism preventatives and in acorns tucked into navels as anti-appendicitis charms.

To the chagrin of the Reverend Adams, Doc refused to warn the local women about their customary morning dosages of Father John's Tonic or Elisha's Elixer.

"If they want a little belt to help them get through the day," said Doc, "why should I interfere with their self-deception? I'd have their consciences in a turmoil if I told them the stuff was stronger than whiskey. Not being damn fools, they know that anyway, but they pretend the alcohol is only there to help dissolve the herbs."

He was far ahead of his time in realizing the fallacy of calling women "the weaker sex."

"If I got to draft somebody to help me take out an appendix on a kitchen table," he said, "I want a woman every time. When the blood starts to flow, a woman is curious about where it comes from and maybe concerned about the waste, but a man will turn green or white and pass out just as you expect him to hand you a clamp."

He said he'd never seen a woman faint at the sight of blood, although he'd seen a lot of them pretend to be about to faint because they had been brought up to believe they were supposed to.

Doc Yates had more chance to observe people in emergencies than did anyone else in town. On a great many of his house calls he couldn't do much more than observe. He could set broken limbs, deliver babies, and perform the few operations doctors dared to tackle at the time, but complex cases defied him.

He could spot more diseases than he could cure. Some of these cured themselves. Doc applied what he called "expectant treatment." He defined this privately as expecting nature to take over.

While he was waiting for this intervention he watched the patient, the family, and the gathered neighbors. He said that it was invariably a man who kept saying, "Doc, why don't you DO something?"

The women, he said, had sense enough to realize that although he wasn't doing much real good he at least wasn't doing any harm, which was more than could be said for Mona Harris with her nettle broth or Aunt Margie with her purges.

Part of Doc's diagnosis was based on his belief that a woman had to be in absolute agony before she would admit that she felt "a little uncomfortable," while a man who had the slightest twinge was liable to say, "Doc, the pain is terrible . . . just terrible."

Doc Yates said that he could see the sex differential assert itself even among the watchers. He said it took strength to be cheerful, resigned, and comforting.

He claimed that while the women were patting pillows or wiping off perspiration or making soup the men would be standing around shaking their heads and saying, "That looks to me like the same thing Ben Murphy, down to Cranston, had and he didn't last three days."

Doc's narrated observations were wasted on most of Cedar River because the observed truths contradicted the old axioms and almost everyone in those days subscribed to the belief that an unfounded statement by a man who was dead had much more validity than did truth voiced by the living, especially if the lie was more poetic. Doc couldn't fight that. His only comfort was the knowledge that, after he died himself, people would start to quote him.

He had no faith in his ability to lead any local crusades in the health field.

Long before I knew him, he had given up trying to stop the traditional use of tobacco juice and spider webs as approved first aid treatment of cuts and gashes. He had even concocted a special lotion for washing away those supposed antiseptics and he could usually remove them rapidly enough to prevent blood poisoning.

Doc was one of the first men in his profession, though, to recognize that part of the physician's duty is to keep the patient's relatives from worrying the patient to death.

As soon as he entered a house, he began assuring everyone in sight that the sick had more salvage possibilities than most men realized.

Doc was no diplomat. He didn't make his comments so that he'd be popular or so the relatives would be relieved. He made them in order to get the household and the gathered neighbors off his back long enough so he could make a decent diagnosis.

It was after the diagnosis that his manner gave real clues about condition. That was the time to watch him.

Sometimes Doc spoke gently and that meant that things were serious. He would give instructions carefully, on those occasions, and he would curse under his breath at the inner knowledge of the fact that almost surely the instructions would be bungled.

He'd say, "You just be sure that Tom gets nothing but the medicine I've left."

The person in attendance would swear obedience on the Bible, on the soul of some dead relative, on hope of Heaven, or on some long-neglected pagan guardian.

Then Doc would go to make another necessary call and some jovial do-gooder like Mona Harris would slide in and overpower the amateur nurse with unbeatable logic.

"We know Doc's stuff is good," Mona would say, "but there ain't no harm in being sure about Tom, is there? What we'll do is give him just a cupful of this tonic that I brewed from dogroots, cress, swampfern."

Fortunately, those times of well-intentioned murder were more rare than the occasions on which Doc could finish his examination and be gruff and tough and so reveal good news.

"How is he, Doc?" my Aunt Margie would ask when Cousin Paul was moaning on the couch from having proved that green grapes were indigestible.

"As well as anyone would expect," Doc would say. "If a billy-goat had eaten half as many, he'd be dead."

"Will Paul be all right?"

"Now, Margie," Doc would answer, "a little unripe fruit won't work miracles. Paul never was quite all right, was he? He's burning in front today, and tomorrow, when you know he's recovered, he'll burn in back. So let's say he'll suffer a couple of days for his sins."

Doc's witticisms on these happy calls would be quoted around town for days. The words were more genteel than people were used to hearing, but they were plain, even when Doc meant them to be subtle.

Subtlety was never in his mind, though, when he had a drink or two with someone whom he credited with common sense and to whom he told, in picturesque profanity, the weaknesses of Cedar River.

On one of those occasions, he told my father the reason for his refusal to move to another town where he might have a better chance to educate the people into an acceptance of what was then modern medicine.

Doc was complaining. My father was agreeing. The question seemed logical and it was asked.

"What I don't understand, Doc," said my father, "is why you've stayed here for so long."

"Well," said Doc, "it's because I enjoy thinking that the world outside of Cedar River is full of hardworking sensible people who pay their bills, think before they act, try to improve themselves, and make sacrifices for posterity."

"That sounds like a reason to leave."

"No," said Doc. "It's a reason to stay. Because I'm almost sure the rest of the world is just as bad as Cedar River. I like to think it isn't but I'm damned sure it is. And if I go out there and see that it is, then I'll lose the pleasure of thinking it's better."

"That's good solid forethought," said my father. "That's sane thinking. You stay here another five years and you can give Euclid a run for his money in the logic line."

Oscar says he doesn't mind.
He says anyone can give him anything.
He says he doesn't mind letting them feel happiness
In return for an old shirt
Or a worn-out pair of shoes.
He says he'll end up with the shirt or shoes
And happiness, too,
Because he MAKES happiness
In a crock.

I don't feel that way.
If they offer me something they'd use,
Something they hate to part with,
Something that's worth something to them,
I'll take it.
I'll thank them.
But the phonies,
The reward in Heaven seekers,
The folks who keep a golden book
Listing their virtuous generosities;
For all of me
They can go to Hell
Still clutching their goddam elbowless overcoats.

—Jonas P. Hall

Chapter II

Vegetable gardens were an important part of life in Cedar River. Every family had one unless the head of the house was willing to advertise thus publicly that he was an outright lazy bum.

Uncle Oscar didn't have a garden but that had no effect on his reputation as a good citizen because nobody ever thought of him as a good citizen anyway.

Jonas Hall didn't have a garden, either. He usually started one but his need to meditate came at odd times and the weeds wouldn't wait.

Reputable people had gardens, however, and that was why Aunt Mavis was a little worried, the spring after she married Uncle Tom, because he was late in doing any garden planning. She questioned him.

"A man that runs a sawmill," said Uncle Tom, "ain't got no time for cucumbers and lettuce and corn and beans."

"You mean, we won't have a garden?" asked Aunt Mavis.

"No. Any spare time I got has to be used for doing work like pouring new bearings on the mandrel shaft or cleaning the carburetor on the mill motor."

"But, people *need* gardens . . . ."

Uncle Tom didn't answer for a minute or two. He had to assemble his words in some decent order. He knew that the need for a garden was a delusion. He also knew that, even had the need been real, a garden was forbidden to him as it was to all sawmill men.

If his sawmill had ever found out that he was planting seeds when he should have been shining and sweeping and shimming, the sawmill would have gone into a frenzy of breaking belt lacings, plugging sawdust carriers, and slipping head dogs. Small sawmills are possessive. They are the most jealous of jealous gods.

Uncle Tom couldn't explain this to Aunt Mavis, though. She still thought a sawmill was an inanimate machine. She didn't know that if a carriage husk knew a sawyer was out thinning beets when the husk needed a comforting oil rub the husk might well throw a mess of steel chips into the sawyer's ear when he stepped into range.

All Tom could do was give Mavis a few words of comfort. He could let her know that there would be produce in plenty, that it would be handed to her when the time came.

"Look," he said, "We won't have the first peas or green beans of the year. But half the people in this town forgets, from season to season, just how many beans grows on a bush and how many cucumbers they can pick from each hill. Don't worry about vegetables, Mavis, just wash your canning jars and wait."

And, in the course of that first canning season, Aunt Mavis came to understand what Uncle Tom meant. Cedar River needed just half the gardens it had. From about the time when the potatoes started to need de-bugging, everybody spent more hours trying to give stuff away than he did harvesting it.

It seemed to Aunt Mavis that she couldn't poke her head out her door without someone saying, "We had some delicious this or that for dinner last night. In a couple of days there'll be a lot more and I'll bring you over some."

The give-away movement picked up momentum as the season advanced. By August, Aunt Mavis was trying to find people to whom to give the beans and peas and corn that had been given to her.

By September, she was getting resigned to the fact that she'd have to fight her way to the porch steps every morning through the piles of tomatoes and cucumbers and chard and shell beans that folks had dumped there in the night.

In October, she started to do a little musing and she delivered an ultimatum to Uncle Tom.

"Next year," she said, "we're going to have a garden even if I have to plant it myself."

Uncle Tom looked at the baskets of tomatoes and cucumbers and squash that filled the kitchen. He thought of the shelves full of canned stuff in the cellar.

"My soul, woman," he said. "What in tunket do we want a garden for? How many pickles do you think we can eat? We'll have to dump the canned vegetables out next August so we'll have the jars to use for the new crops . . . ."

"That's just it," said Aunt Mavis. "It seems as though I've spent the whole summer canning. And neither of us really likes vegetables well enough to eat two quarts apiece every day."

"So why grow more?"

"Because, " she said, "if we have even three rows of something or other, then folks can't say we don't have a garden of our own. We won't be fair game, that way, for people who don't want to waste things."

"You might be right," said Uncle Tom. "You just might be absolutely right . . . we'll have to do *something* . . . ."

That winter, he thought of the solution. He bought a woodlot ten miles out of town and moved. The timber wasn't as good as what he'd been cutting and sawing, but the distance discouraged folks from bringing him their surplus garden truck and thus getting the warm glow of do-gooderism at his expense.

There was a poet years ago who said
No man was truly happy
If he got a fortune in the mail,
Unless the next letter told about
Some friend who had gone bankrupt.

In Cedar River, that would be pure nonsense.
The bankrupt man and every other man in town
Would put the buzz on him that got the fortune;
Sad story him and swindle him and con him;
Strip the poor guy clean;
Leave him maybe fifteen cents
To buy a Thank You card.

There's no point here in wishing hardship
Or bad luck or poverty
On someone else.
In this town, he'll find a way to share it.

—Jonas P. Hall

Chapter III

The spirit of civilization was always kept fairly well at bay by the reluctance of Cedar River people to abandon the comfortable philosophies of primitive economic and social codes.

Our town was always willing to subsidize the needy. Sometimes this was done joyfully, as when the town tendered its subsidy to Fishbait Olson with a march and a party that almost bankrupted the subsidized family.

Fishbait Olson sprained his ankle. The neighbors decided to help him out with food, not sent in some coldly charitable way but carried in friendship by a sizable group. Naturally, Mrs. Olson felt she must offer the donors some refreshment and somehow she ended up by cooking all the food they brought and also all she had left in her own larder.

Old Fishbait had to cripple out the next morning and shoot a deer so his family could eat while he was being an invalid.

But the motivations were pure. The end result was not planned, but accidental. The Olsons understood that.

People who didn't try to help themselves solve problems, however, didn't get any help at all from neighbors. If people tried and still couldn't cope, they got prodding as well as help. That same attitude prevailed in Mrs. Kelly's school.

Stupidity in our classroom, if it were recognized by Mrs. Kelly as real stupidity, might soften the blows for non-achievement, but some blows were still given. They helped a stupid boy to try to help himself.

Even the temporary presence of temporary physical disability called for nothing more than an adjustment of target or some instruction in self-protection.

My cousin Paul once pleaded invalidism when Mrs. Kelly drew back her hand to correct his addition of Pennsylvania to the list of states in the corn belt.

"Please, Mrs. Kelly," he said. "I've got a loose tooth."

She hesitated a moment. Then she said, "Don't swallow it if you feel it on your tongue. Spit it out. If it goes down in your stomach, it could churn around and make a hole. You don't want a hole in your stomach, do you?"

"No, Mrs. Kelly," said Paul.

That warning having been given, she smacked him hard on the side of the head. When he couldn't produce the tooth, she smacked him on the other side. The tooth popped out, painless dentistry thus achieved by counter pain.

One of Mrs. Kelly's habits made our education a constant competition. We didn't fight for the highest grade but we did fight against getting the lowest grade. The scholar who got the lowest grade was given special attention and this attention was not the same as is given now to the "under-achievers."

Our schoolhouse rivalries followed us outside. We ran races against each other. We had informal exaggeration contests involving the amount of wood we had stacked or the number of fish we had caught. We competed in the rashness of the harebrained stunts we would pull in "follow the leader."

But although we were always rivals, we did try to help the most dim-witted in "hide and seek." We tried to make sure that some blunderer was not invariably "it." And we were really happy when some stroke of good fortune hit one of our group.

In this happiness we were sincere. We didn't merely pretend happiness in the manner of a group of corporation executives who congratulate a fellow employee on a promotion but secretly wish he'd drown in the bathtub before midnight.

We meant it when we said, "Gee, that's great."

The exception to this was Florence Coosterman. Florence was thirty years ahead of her times in guile, in contest tactics, in subterfuge, and in vision. She was a child prodigy who recognized her own abilities and she probably had legitimate reasons for feeling that all honors belonged rightly to her and that justice was distorted when someone less worthy than herself was favored.

Florence thought she should win all the time. When she didn't win, she did her best to bring a winning classmate down from his dream cloud faster than a chopper can cut the foundations of security out from under a treed coon.

She was always particularly bitter when someone she knew to be her proven inferior got ahead of her by some malicious twist of fortune. That happened to Bobby Seekings.

Bobby came to school one morning and announced a bit of impending glory. He was bubbling. We gathered around him in the schoolyard while he told us that his father had been left some money by a relative in Boston. I forget how much money it was but I know it was an impressive amount, maybe two thousand dollars or more.

We formed a line and shook hands with the son of the blessed heir. We told him how proud we were to have the son of an heir in our school. We told him we hoped he'd still speak to us.

In these actions we were half-joking and half-serious. But we became completely serious when Bobby said his father was going to Boston to get the money and that Bobby had been told that if he behaved himself prior to the trip he could go along.

The idea of Bobby going off to Boston impressed us all much more than the fact of Bobby's father getting some money. A sum of money like that was more than a sixth grade imagination could deal with. But we could all appreciate the value of a train trip to Boston, staying overnight at least, maybe going to a ball game, eating in a hotel.

We lined up and shook hands again. This time, though, Florence Coosterman couldn't make it. She stood a few steps away, biting her lips. Then, as though someone had jabbed her with a joy needle, she brightened.

"Have you got a sheep to take with you?" she asked.

"A sheep?" asked Bobby.

"Yes," said Florence. "You'd better pick out a small one to take along. At least I would if I were you. I don't think there are many sheep down there and I have a feeling you'll need a sheep."

"What would he need a sheep for?" I asked. "Boston is full of restaurants. There must be a million restaurants in Boston. You think he'll have to build a fire and cook a sheep?"

"You would be the one to think about food," she said. "The sheep is for a subsitute sacrifice. Don't you read the Bible?"

"Sure, I do," I said. "I guess I haven't read all of it but I've read a lot of it. What's that got to do with Bobby?"

"If you had read the parts that you should have read," said Florence, "you'd know that good people who get special blessings always offer sacrifices. They cut something open and offer it on an altar. The usual thing is to cut open the oldest son."

Bobby paled. Being the only son, he qualified. "My father wouldn't cut me open," he said. "You're crazy."

"He would if there wasn't a sheep handy," she said. "Your father's as good as Abraham, isn't he? Well, that was what Abraham was going to do. He was going to push a knife into his son to show how thankful he was for his blessings. He was going to twist it and turn it and probably cut his son's heart out. But then he saw this sheep and he cut it open instead."

"You're making all that up . . ."

"No, she isn't," said Pete Baker. "That's all in the Bible. But I didn't think people did it anymore."

"Good people do," said Florence. "And Bobby's father is a good man, so he will. We don't know about things like that because nobody around here ever had any big blessings before this one. You can do what you want to do, Bobby, but I wouldn't even think of going to Boston if I were you . . . not unless I took a sheep."

"Golly," said Bobby.

"Of course, you might want to be cut open for a sacrifice," said Florence. "I wouldn't, but you might. You're just dumb enough to."

The bell rang. We filed into school.

Through the next week, Bobby never mentioned Boston. Then, one afternoon, Bobby's father was sitting on our front porch when I got home. He was talking to my father and I heard a few sentences.

"Wish I could have taken the boy, " he said, "but, George, I swear he's getting feeble minded. He hollered and yelled and said he wouldn't go if he couldn't take a sheep along."

"A what?"

"A sheep. How do you figure that one out?"

"No figuring to it," said my father.

But there was, and the figure had to be added to Florence's already one-sided score.

Mrs. Turner lectured Oscar on the evils brewed
In vats with alcohol.
"You jeopardize your soul," she said.
"You wreck the reputation of the town.
All across the state, good people shudder
When we tell them where we come from."

Oscar said, "Do you folks ever wonder if
You might not be confusing
My personal salvation with your social aims?"

—Jonas P. Hall

Chapter IV

My uncle Oscar was one of the only men I ever knew who recognized the extent to which most people deceive themselves in order to reconcile conscience with happiness. If he hadn't recognized that, he might have followed their example. That would have been a deadly thing, actually, because as a solid citizen he would have been a bore and a blithering nuisance.

My father told Oscar just that on the one occasion when it seemed possible that he had decided to forsake rascality. He jolted my father. That was unusual. My father was ordinarily able to accept changes in men as casually as he accepted changes in the wind or the river level.

It was my mother who alerted my father to the signs of Uncle Oscar's strangeness. She had been to the Tuesday night session of Protracted Meeting Week, the annual soul saving crusade that was a feature of every rural town when I was a boy.

My father didn't hold with annual revivals. He said he was

damned if he was going to spend even one of the six scheduled nights listening to an imaginative evangelist describe the Hell that folks would see for themselves if they didn't behave and shouldn't be impressed by if they did.

He said his stomach couldn't stand the sight of a bunch of emotional people vowing in public that they were going to start living the kind of lives they had been previously pretending to live.

My mother knew how he felt so she didn't comment on the sermon. She gave him the important news instead.

"Oscar was there," she said.

"Probably thought he was going to a girlie show," said my father. "Didn't stay long, I'll bet."

"Yes he did. He sat all through it and he joined in the 'Amens' too. Mr. Reynolds thought he was drinking but he went over and talked with him and then he shook hands with him and left him alone. George, do you think . . .?"

"No, I don't. He didn't go up and get saved, did he?"

"He could be just waiting until Saturday," said my mother. "Almost everyone waits until Saturday. There's more of a crowd to hear the sins confessed."

"Oscar's should draw a record crowd," said my father.

In spite of this pretended casualness, though, my father made a point of finding Oscar the next day. Usually such a search involved much wandering around, because Oscar didn't live any kind of a patterned life. But my father found Oscar right on the store steps. Oscar was scrubbed and shaved.

"What do you think you're doing?" asked my father.

"Nothing wrong," said Oscar. "I'm just sitting here musing on the wickedness of the world."

"I don't mean now. I mean last night. I mean, you went to the services last night . . . ."

"Yeah."

"How did you decide that would be an entertaining activity?"

"George," said Oscar, "don't jeopardize your soul by making jokes about salvation."

"Shut up. You know you're making a fool of yourself."

"Can't help that. The urge to repent is in me, George. I'm going to repent and be a new man."

My father left him and went to the parsonage. The Reverend Adams was interested but claimed neutrality.

"You know I don't approve of these dramatic revivalists," he said, "But there's no way to keep them out of town and if they come to town there's no way to keep people from supporting them."

"I'm not talking about supporting them," said my father. "I'm talking about people shouting their way toward the golden stairs when some showman prods them with a few volts of piety."

"There's nothing I can do about it. These annual orgies are traditional. Besides, a few sermons won't hurt Oscar."

"They won't help him either. Oscar does more for the happiness of this town by being a picturesque scoundrel than he would if he became a stupid saint."

"I might agree with that last remark," said the minister, "except that you'd quote me . . . so I won't."

My father gave up. Uncle Oscar sat silently on the store steps all day, tipping his hat to passing ladies and pretending to ignore their quick sidesteps. He even turned down a free bite of Francis Gage's plug of tobacco, but that might have been more in the interest of hygiene than in hopes of a smile from Heaven.

He went to services that night, too, and he alarmed Uncle Waldron. Waldron had been bludgeoned into attendance by Aunt Margie. He sat right on the edge of the bench, eyes on Oscar, breathing as deeply as he would have if he were watching a fall moose.

Waldron could hardly wait until he'd finished his tenth pancake the next morning before he ran over to our house.

"You got to do something, George," he said. "Oscar was at the revival last night and he kept clearing his throat as though he was going to get up and confess a few things."

"How would that hurt you?"

"Well, George, nobody knows just what Oscar might confess."

"You mean the sins might not have been solitary," said my father. "Yes, I can see where that might be a hazard. Well, I'll talk to him again."

Oscar was once more ensconced on the store steps. He nodded gravely to my father, but my father wasn't being polite.

"You damn fool," said my father, "you're scaring the innards out of the righteous. You let yourself get pious enough to start disclosing your transgressions and somebody's going to shoot you to shut you up."

"I got to take that chance," said Oscar.

"Why? Listen . . . you know you don't have any intention of leading a sinless life after Saturday night, even if you were going to live any life . . . which I'm not sure you're going to . Oscar, have you been to a doctor? Are you sick or something?"

"Matter of fact," said Oscar, "I ain't too well. But that's not why I think I ought to repent."

"Malarky. You know that's malarky. There's nothing like a sick spell to send a sinner toward salvation. What's wrong? What did you find out? How are you sick?"

"I got palpalooshians. But, George, even if I was well, I'd want to start a better life."

"If you were well and healthy, you'd be starting a batch of brew. Oscar, you're not talking to some dumbhead. You're talking to a man that's known you for thirty-odd years. Palpalooshians your foot. I never heard of palpalooshians."

"They're painful, George. My arteries pound in my head. I can hear them pound when I lie down at night."

"Arteries," said my father, "are tubes. They can't pound."

"Steam lines are tubes and they pound."

"That's condensate and you know it. Your arteries aren't full of condensate . . . well, maybe yours are, at that. Oscar, how about some straight answers? You got heart trouble? Is that what Doc said?"

"I ain't been to Doc. I don't need him. I know what I got. I got palpalooshians and when a man's got palpalooshians he's got two choices. He can get ready to meet his maker, clear his conscience by disclosing his sins and naming his companions in sin, or he can try to raise enough money to go to Cranston and get cured."

"Cranston is only 10 miles downriver," said my father. "You can go for 50 cents on the mail truck. Oscar, how much does the cure cost? Who knows how to cure whatever you've got in Cranston?"

"It's a simple cure," said Oscar. "It's just rest and recreation and relief of tensions. It just takes a few days of soothing your nerves. But if a man can't afford it . . . well . . . . "

"Oh. I think . . . oh . . . "

"Yeah. So if you should happen to meet Waldron when you go back to report to him . . . . "

"That's a stupid way to put it."

"It is, ain't it? Well, if you should happen to report to him when he comes to see you, you tell him that Deak Trembley and Jeb Seekings and Luther Haley has already decided to kick in ten bucks to get me cured instead of hearing me get publicly saved and tell who I was sinning with. That's thirty and I need forty."

My father grinned. "You damned old thief," he said.

Oscar grinned back. "I ain't so very old," he answered. "In fact, if you wasn't going to be deprived of hearing me confess, you wouldn't think I was old at all."

Four years ago,
Herb Shorey's wife left him.
She went home to her mother.

Since then,
Herb has been saying,
"I find my solace
In the fact
That Sally's probably happier
Where she is."

Last week,
Sally's mother called to say
That Sally was on her way back.
Herb hung up the phone and screamed,
"Now, where in hell
Am I going to find solace for THAT?"

—Jonas P. Hall

Chapter V

Maxine Thomas was Cedar River's finest example of a tolerant woman. She lived uncomplainingly with the obvious faults of a husband to whom she had promised loyalty in her marriage vows. This was unusual conduct.

Many Cedar River wives had husbands who were forty miles from the first signpost on the road to perfection. But these husbands were kept informed of their deficiencies, vocally or physically. Maxine Thomas didn't nag her husband or throw crockery at him or even try to change his ways by sleeping on the kitchen couch.

She made occasional suggestions about remedies for faults, but when he seemed perplexed to hear that he was less than he should be, Maxine kissed him and told him not to worry, because she loved him.

Actually, Benny Thomas didn't have too many faults. His big problem was that he wasn't very smart and even a vigorous correction expert like Aunt Margie couldn't have done anything about that. Margie would have straightened out his priorities, though. She would have taught him to pay more attention to neatness and less to being clumsily lovable.

Benny was one of the most religious men in town. He should have known that cleanliness was next to godliness. But he embraced the latter and scorned the former. He was sloppy, untidy, and a home-front litterbug.

Benny Thomas' idea of a neat yard was one through which an alert kangaroo could hop without hitting more than three discarded oil cans.

His motions toward personal grooming consisted of making a few frantic passes with a washcloth over his anatomy on Saturday nights. He combed his hair with his fingers. His face, after shaving, looked like a hand mown hayfield on which some drunk had swung the scythe while being chased by bees.

When the Thomas family went to prayer meeting, Benny spoke loudly of the need to cleanse souls from sin. Maxine listened to his pleadings but she wished that he might be a little more concerned about the grime under his fingernails.

After five years of marriage, Maxine found herself unable to see the fence line for the junk. Benny had reached a certain stage of ripeness and somehow managed to hold to that condition and thus keep himself from absolute decay.

Maxine prayed and got her answer.

She announced one day at breakfast that cleaning up was the order of the moment. Her reason was unchallengeable.

"Benny," she said, "you've told me many times that people should think of their souls instead of their surroundings . . . ."

"That's right," said Benny. "If folks would spend more time praying and less time painting, their future in heaven would be secure even if their houses decayed a little. My father used to say, Maxine, that you can get rid of your sins in the bliss of repentance but you can't wash them off in the bathtub."

There were many women in town who would have pointed out that Benny's father had not been an authority on bathtubs, never having had one and never having given any indication that he was sad because of his deprivation.

But Maxine only smiled. "I agree with all that," she said, "but today is a special day. Benny, I've had a revelation. Tonight at eight o'clock, the world is going to end and the Lord is going to pick up the chosen in his chariots of fire. We're going to be ready for him."

A less devout man than Benny might have challenged the truth of his wife's prophecy. But Benny believed. To fail in belief would have been to deny the fundamentalism which rested solidly in his innocent mind. He stood up.

"We'd better start praying," he said.

"You know better than that," said Maxine.

"Know better than to pray?"

"Know better than to think it will do any good. You told me long ago that those who put their hopes for salvation on a few fast prayers on judgment day would be waiting too long and would be herded with the condemned."

Benny stared at her in puzzled inactivity. "What *are* we going to do?" he asked.

"First, we're going to clean the yard. Benny, how do you think a chariot is going to find a landing place in all that clutter? A wheel would catch in an old car fender or something and the chariot would tip over."

"It could land in the road."

"Nonsense. It if did, then all the lost souls would try to climb aboard. We wouldn't get even close to it."

"I guess that's right."

"I know it's right. So we clean the yard and then the house and then ourselves. When eight o'clock comes, I'm going to meet my maker in a spotless dress in a spotless parlor.

"Yeah. Me, too. Have I got some clean clothes?"

"Certainly. Now we'll start hauling junk and then we'll beat the carpets and scrub down the walls. I want the fence straightened up, too, and the steps repaired."

Benny took off his shirt and went to work. Spurred by the approach of the hour for which he had been preparing his soul for years, he cleaned with the vigor of a madman and intensity of a drowning swimmer struggling for the safety of the shore.

By six-thirty, the premises were awesome in their tidiness. By eight o'clock, Benny and Maxine and the two children were waiting in the parlor, their skin smarting from their scrubbing.

By ten o'clock, the children were fast asleep. Benny was yawning between his shorter and shorter prayers. Maxine rose.

"I guess I must have misunderstood," she said. "I know I heard the day of the week and the time right. It was Saturday night at eight o'clock. So that part is certain. I guess it's the week that I didn't hear correctly . . . maybe the year. Well, it doesn't matter."

"It doesn't matter?" asked Benny, his confusion now three times as great as it had been at breakfast time. "Maxine, why doesn't it matter?"

"Because now we know the day and the hour. All we have to do is spend every Saturday cleaning up the place and us."

"Every Saturday?"

"Of course. We certainly want to be prepared when the right day comes."

"My soul," said Benny. "My *soul* . . . ."

"Yes," said Maxine. "Aren't we lucky that we know just exactly what day to get ready for the angels who will come to save it!"

Cedar River Folks don't prove the strength
Of heredity
Or of environment, either.
Like everybody else,
They prove
That if we don't watch ourselves
Every damn minute,
We'll become what we behold.

Why should scholars care
Whether it's example or breeding
That makes us poorer specimens
Than we should be?

Do they think they can change
The editorial content
Of the magazine of misdeeds?

—Jonas P. Hall

Chapter VI

There never was nor will there be again a place like Turner's Store on a Saturday afternoon thirty years ago. The store is still there but it is not the store it was. It lacks the smells that cannot seep through packages and the less definable ones that are now deodorants.

The old store smelled of dogs and leather and alcohol illicit. It smelled of fresh ground coffee, now contained in cans. It smelled of stable boots unwiped and pipes that had to be set down outdoors between periods allowed by custom for their use while tender-stomached men threw cedar shavings on the stove and breathed that smoke in preference.

It's a good store still, but refinement has removed the shavings box which spitters missed as often as they hit. A creed less tolerant of folks who help themselves has stopped the sale of crackers from the open barrels, not because old Turner fears the germs that might be thus invited but because he knows that modern cracker losses would become a major item.

The clubroom atmosphere is now sporadic. That's to be expected. If the government had found out that the store was being used for village recreation, other forum sites not conscientiously provided by the taxpayers of the town, a grant would have been forced on the selectmen and a fancy building put up to stand empty and remind the people that their lack of needless things was greater than it should be.

Turner's Store on Saturday was good enough. That's where the men were gathered when the stranger came to straighten out the records of his research.

The stranger was soft-spoken, mild-mannered, physically small. He looked like a scholar. He wore heavy glasses and he carried a pencil and a notebook.

He stimulated both mental and physical activity when he showed up at Cedar River Saturday assembly time.

Uncle Oscar provided the physical activity. He ducked out the back door. He didn't care for strangers, however garbed or innocent appearing or casual seeming. He knew that any stranger could turn out to be a trapper, sent by snoops to interfere with men who tried to make themselves a drink or two and so remove the burden of their drink provision from the national economy.

The other loungers in the store adjusted their minds to cope with a census taker, a tax checker, a lawyer for someone who had fallen down in the street, or a salesman of whatever they needed least.

They didn't worry about just which of these occupations was represented by the stranger. There was no difference in the traditional treatment. Cedar River men lied to them all, not viciously but routinely and protectively and sometimes sadly.

It turned out, though, that this Saturday stranger was a historian. He was compiling facts about the upper river and he'd been reading back files of the *Cranston Gazette*. He was confused. He wanted to ask some questions.

The loungers catalogued him as harmless. They told him to sit down. They let him buy them cigars from Mr. Turner's special box, the one that was marked "De-Luxe Delights—25¢."

Some passing politician had discarded that box, years before. Mr. Turner always kept it half-full of his regular five-centers for times like this when thoughtful preparation paid off.

The men didn't grudge Mr. Turner this extra profit. He was providing heat and shelter. He was entitled to rent as long as the rent money came from an outsider.

After the cigars were lighted, the stranger revealed his confusion. It was understandable. His trouble was that he wanted to be accurate in his chronicle of the river towns. That was hard because, in the old newspaper files, he had kept running into obituaries and reminiscences that seemed to contradict vital records, possibilities, and logic.

This was particularly true of Cedar River. The birth, marriage, anniversary, and death notices sent to the paper from our town were written by people who were discreet and kind. Thus truth was subordinated to the feelings of the families.

"I've got a list here," said the stranger, "of things I'd like to straighten out if I possibly could. Here's an obituary of a man named Ralph Trembley. Did any of you know him?"

"Deak's uncle," said Jeb Seekings.

"No," said Deak. "He was a kind of second cousin. I never really knowed him. He died just a while after I was born."

"The date is 1908," said the stranger, "and he was supposed to be fifty-six years old, but it says here that his father was a Revolutionary War colonel . . ."

"Well," said Deak, "Ralph always told that. It wasn't true, of course, but his wife felt good when it came out in the paper. It kinda gave a little importance to the family. And there wasn't nothing much else to print about Ralph."

The historian looked startled, but he made a note and turned the page in his book. "Here are six more obituaries," he said, "and each one names a different man as an ancestor, but each says that the ancestor was the first settler in Cedar River. That's an important point in town history. Who *was* the first settler here?"

"Who cares?" asked Jonas Hall. "Mister, there's always been an argument about that. I don't know why settling Cedar River was anything to be proud of, but an obituary doesn't seem to be a proper place for debate over seniority."

"But we have to respect facts, man," said the historian. "We can't record fairy stories and call them history."

"Why not? If poets wrote history and changed it some, people might be prouder of what the world has been. Who would that hurt?"

"It would certainly hurt the serious probers into the past."

"People who probe into Cedar River's past," said Jonas, "are much more likely to be hurt if they come across the truth than if they read the nice things we put in our records."

"But after a person is dead, his errors are forgiven."

Jonas shook his head. "That may help his soul," he admitted. "I guess I'm willing to agree that it might, even though I never believed that it should. A man's soul is with him all the time he's sinning and it hardly seems fair that after he's dead the soul can fly up there and say it's sorry and have the gates opened. But that's all right. I'm not arguing about that."

"I'm having trouble," said the historian, "in figuring out exactly what you are arguing about. Truth is truth, right? A man does certain things, right? So they're on his records."

"Not here, they ain't," said Jeb Seekings. "At least I don't want to catch no town clerk sending out information about old Bart, my grandfather. You can say his errors are forgiven, but my wife would never forgive me if I let some snoop list them in a book someplace so folks could sing about them to my children."

"Never in my life," said the historian, "have I heard such nonsense. You might just as well lie about people on their tombstones."

"I don't know what kind of an impolite town you come from," said Jonas Hall. "Tombstones here are the business of the families of the dead. Whatever they want to say, we let them say. I suppose there aren't half the tombstones in our cemetery that tell the absolute truth."

"You'd lie on a tombstone? You really would?"

"Not on mine," said Jonas. "I don't have a family and I try to keep track of my age, give or take a couple of years. But there's Mrs. Peters, for instance. Sweet lady. Never hurt anybody. I happen to know how old she is. But she's been dropping a year off here and there for as long as I can remember. Took her through four hunting seasons to go from 39 to 40. So, right now she thinks she's 59."

The historian smiled. "Those things happen," he said.

"Yeah, but here we see to it that they stay happened if you see what I mean. Suppose while she's still telling everyone she's 70, she happens to die. We going to make a liar out of her by putting dates on her stone that claim she was 81, which she would be if she said she was 70?"

The historian looked at Jonas. He looked at Jeb Seekings, who was nodding in agreement. He looked at the floor as though he expected a beetle to poke its head out and say, "My family has been here since 1453."

Deak Trembley cleared his throat. "Was there some other facts you wanted to check up on, Mister?" he asked.

"Facts? The only fact I have is that there are no facts. I don't know what kind of a town history is ever going to be written about this place . . ."

"A kind one, I hope," said Jonas.

"History is not supposed to be . . ." began the historian. "Oh the hell with it."

The door slammed as he left. Jeb Seekings looked at Jonas. "Do you really mean that Mrs. Peters has managed to skip 12 years so far?" he asked.

"Of course not," said Jonas. "I don't suppose it's more than four or five. But I always believed a person should put himself out a little to make history more dramatic. In school, I found it dull."

A woman doesn't need to want a certain man,
To be jealous of the friend
That gets him.
No, indeed.
Not any more than prohibitionists
Want the drink
They're pledged to keep their brothers
From enjoying.

The woman owes it to her pride
To interfere.
The prohibitionists just hate
Enjoyment.

—Jonas P. Hall

Chapter VII

It was the season of the re-birth, of the stirring of nature after the winter which had been much too long. In the swamps the first small figures were blooming unnoticed. In the hidden patches at the edges of the clearings, the arbutus was waiting.

As nature stirred, so stirred the boys of Cedar River. We heard the peepers in the dusk and we noted the presence of new birds which stayed in the area only long enough to rest and feed and fly on toward their summer grounds. We felt winter's weight leave us as the frost leaves the balsam.

To a Cedar River boy in the summer, there was freedom of action, unlimited except by lack of ideas and by dictated sessions with a hoe and a hay rake. In the fall, there was sadness and the preparation for a period of confinement. In the winter, there was only a stubborn determination to stay alive until spring despite Mrs. Kelly's school, and snow shoveling, and the carrying of cords of wood.

But in the spring, the promises of a refreshed world brought emotions surging so close to the surface that laughter and love were constantly threatening release or declaration.

It was suitable and right and fitting that Sally Reynolds should come to Cedar River in the spring. She must have come riding on a cloud, because we always took note of traffic and no one saw the manner of her conveyance. She was just suddenly there.

Sally Reynolds was a blonde glory in a pink dress and white stockings and black sandals. She sat demurely on the steps of Turner's Store. She smiled, but the smile was distant. She glowed, and the glow was stimulus for each boy's analysis of his own unworthiness for the friendship of such a goddess.

We were twelve years old and we possessed no fit offerings to lay at Sally's feet. We had found no fame and won no laurels. We had nothing to give but ourselves and we knew that wasn't much.

"Who is she?" I asked Ned Trembley.

"Sally Reynolds," he said. "She's Mrs. Turner's niece. Her father's sick. She's going to stay awhile. Mrs. Turner told my mother she was coming. Gee, she's pretty. I'd like to meet her."

"I ain't afraid to talk to her," said my cousin Paul.

"Why don't you, then?" asked Ned.

"I don't want to," said Paul, but the rapturous look on his face denied his words. "I got nothing to talk about," he added.

"She's probably just waiting for someone to be friendly," said Ned. "Hey, there's Florence . . . Come here . . . . Listen, we want to meet that girl on the steps. You could go make friends with her and then we could walk over and you could introduce us."

Florence was no do-gooder. "What'll you give me?" she asked.

We argued and accused and finally settled on five cents apiece. Florence collected in advance. Ned stated the specifics.

"Remember, now," he said. "You introduce us properly."

"I'm familiar with the forms of politeness," said Florence.

She walked over and sat down beside Sally. We gave her two minutes to make friends. Then we formed a row by the steps.

"Oh, Sally," said Florence. "I'm delighted to introduce you to these boys. May I present Paul Dodds? He's the dopey looking droopy-pants on the end. He looks like what he is. He's stupid."

"Hey," said Paul. *"Hey!"*

"See?" said Florence. "He's always thinking about food, too."

"Florence . . . ." protested Ned Trembley.

"I'm getting to you," said Florence. "Don't rush me. Sally, may I also present Neddy-Boy Trembley. You can remember him easily. He always smells as though he washed in old garbage."

Ned wilted. "Judas, Joe, Jumping Darn," he said.

"He swears," said Florence. "He's evil incarnated."

I grabbed Ned and started to retreat. Florence screamed in her triumph. "Don't hurry, Billy," she said. "You'll lose your nickel. Sally, the one that's running . . . that's Billy Clark . . . he's a heathen relative of rum drinkers and he punches girls in the stomach . . . Billy . . . Oh, ha, ha, ha . . ."

As we ran, Ned swore some more. "Someday," he said, "I'll get that Florence. I'll get her good."

"I hope so," I said. "I hope somebody does. It won't be me. I've given up trying."

"We'll never get near that girl now," said Paul.

"Not unless there's a miracle," said Ned, "and I don't believe in those any more."

But the miracle came. Three days after our first glimpse of the visiting goddess, she walked over to Ned Trembley and started to talk. When I saw what had happened, I headed for the scene at a straight gallop. Cousin Paul followed me.

"She says she's tired of Florence bossing her around," said Ned. "She says Florence doesn't want her to have any fun."

"She certainly doesn't want me to meet any *boys*," said Sally.

"You're meeting some now," said Paul. "Hey, look, I can stand on my head."

"Well, well, well," said a nasal voice. "So the vultures gather around their victim."

We turned. Florence Coosterman was smirking at us.

"You can't learn that you're obnoxious, can you?" she asked. "You have to force yourselves on people, don't you?"

Sally spoke up. "I wanted to talk to them, Florence," she said. "I'm not going to go back home without meeting anybody except YOU. I think they're nice boys . . . all of them.

"Yawh-Haw," said Cousin Paul to Florence.

"Nice boys," said Florence, "with a nice pet donkey. I'm sure you don't want to miss all that just to learn the secret of concentrated June dew as a beauty salve. So I'll go alone."

"Wait," said Sally. "You know a secret beauty salve?"

"Yes, but you're busy with the boys and it has to be today."

"I can see the boys later," said Sally. "Can't I, boys?"

We assured her that she could. We said we'd see her by the store after supper. As she walked away with Florence, we grew tall with the tonic of romance in prospect. We goggled and glowed.

I refused an extra pudding at supper. "I'm going to get cleaned up and walk down to the store," I said.

"Cleaned up?" asked my father. "Voluntarily?"

I feared a few questions, but my father had reminded himself of something. He laughed at the memory. He laughed heartily.

"Mrs. Turner sure had a cleaning up job this afternoon on that niece of hers," he said. "Holy Moses, what a mess that must have been. The girl had hysterics. She's on her way back to the city right now. Mrs. Turner had to start right off with her . . ."

I stood in a semi-shock. My father kept laughing. He spoke in garbled gasps between his unrestricted chuckles.

"That girl must be a lunatic. She rubbed her face and hair . . . she said somebody told her that June dew gathered in magic circles of green grass and then was . . . was concentrated by the sun . . . and . . . it would make her *beautiful* . . . Dear Joshua . . . *Beautiful* . . . ."

"She rubbed her face in *what*?" I asked.

"What do you think is circled by green grass in a June cow pasture?" asked my father. "She said she was told to rub it on *Good*."

"That was Florence Coosterman told her that," I yelled. "It isn't funny at all and it's *mean* to laugh about it."

My father stopped laughing. "So," he said. "That was the way the tree was toppling. I didn't know. I'm sorry, Bill."

Then he smiled again. "After you calm down," he said, "You might be thanking Florence, though. Suppose this had gone along and become serious. Pretty or not, Bill, a man is lucky to be saved from marrying a woman that doesn't know concentrated June dew from cow dung. Think of what she might cook for breakfast."

That set him off into another gale. I stood there, hating life.

If it's your town, you can run it.
You can classify your neighbors,
Fill out their social rating cards,
Stack the deck.

You know who ought to win,
Who ought to lose.
You have a right to set the rules,
Saying, "I always deal,
Nobody cuts,
Nobody shuffles."

It's all pat, all neat, all tidy,
As long as you remember every night,
To search the guests for jokers.

—*Jonas P. Hall*

Chapter VIII

Absolute equality destroys pleasure. When each man is as good as another, then no one can be better than anyone else. This is a bitter situation in practice, even though it might not be so defined in democratic theory. Most people are sad when they have no one to look up to and even sadder when they have no one to look down on.

Cedar River never had that problem. It had definite degrees of non-importance. It had people who were mildly useless, people who were completely useless, and people who destroyed the usefulness of other people by their drain on the values given.

Even the Cedar River outcasts, however, scorned by everyone in town, could still feel superior to the residents of Big Brook. Most of them weren't superior but they felt superior and, since superiority is nine-tenths delusion and one-tenth scorn of reality known, the feeling is normally the equivalent of the being.

Except for my uncle Oscar, who was a lost sheep in reputation and in deed, the Cedar River people had positive ideas about Big Brookers. The fewer Big Brookers they had met, the more positive were their ideas. Actually, it was hard for any decent citizen to meet a Big Brooker because the very act of meeting destroyed some part of the aura of decency.

Most of the knowledge about Big Brookers was, therefore, a myth, but it was one that most Cedar River people would swear was truth.

Big Brookers were outlanders and probably outlaws. They were rough, coarse, and mostly illiterate. They lived in semi-isolation and they were suspicious of strangers. They were dirty, they intermarried, they were uncouth.

Believing all this, some of which might even have been true, Cedar River women locked their doors when Big Brookers came to town to trade. Storekeepers, barbers, blacksmiths, and grain dealers, with Christian love, raised their prices to penalize this horde of the ungodly.

When Cedar River men got into an argument, the final insult that indicated a desire for physical blows was the statement, "You act as though you was brought up in Big Brook." After that, there was no turning back. Blood had to flow before honor was satisfied.

In the social structure of Cedar River itself, the castes were formed around occupation, education, church attendance, bad habits, and family ties. The structure was fluid and different citizens assigned different ratings to the same individuals. The only thing that was definitely agreed on was that Mrs. Turner stood or sat on the top of the social heap.

The Turners owned the store. They were creditors to almost everyone in town. They were neutral in church feuds and they bought a new Buick each year. All these things combined to give Mrs. Turner the nod. She edited the unpublished social guide. She was the arbiter of degree, the judge of acceptability.

So there was no problem of acceptance when Mrs. Turner brought a sweet-looking young lady to the weekly sewing circle.

"This is Cora Nelson," said Mrs. Turner. "She's rooming with us for awhile . . . . until she can make other arrangements."

There wasn't much sewing that afternoon. The ladies were more interested in statistics than in stitches. Some probed at Cora and some probed at Mrs. Turner. Everyone went home with a stock of information and that stock was spread promptly by telephone. Before sunset, the whole town knew Cora's story.

Cora Nelson was 23 years old. She had arrived on the mail stage from Cranston two days before Mrs. Turner brought her to the sewing circle. Her parents had been killed in a train wreck, a fearful catastrophe in which Cora's life had been spared because she happened to be in the dining car at the time of the crash.

She had fought her way through the wreckage to her parents and before her father died he told her to find a small town where friendly people would protect her. She had chosen Cedar River.

"She's a sweet thing," said Mrs. Turner. "She has pictures of her father and her mother on her dresser. Anyone whose parents were as genteel-looking as hers . . . . well, I always say that it's easy to tell good blood lines . . . they show themselves to the discerning. This girl has good blood."

My mother relayed this remark to my father and my father was amused enough to comment on it to Doc Yates. Doc snorted.

"I don't know what 'good' means when you apply it to blood," said Doc. "I don't suppose it would amuse Mrs. Turner, though, if I told her that the best from a health standpoint is pretty well monopolized by the Gages in this town. Their blood is red, rich, and racing."

Doc was the only one who challenged Mrs. Turner's meaning. To the upper social strata, good blood meant gentility. They weren't puzzled about the meaning of the phrase "until she makes other arrangements," either. The eligible bachelors began to call.

Six weeks from the day she came to town, Cora Nelson married Bud Growder. Bud ran the excelsior mill. He qualified financially and socially. His father was a teller in the Cranston bank. His mother had been to normal school. Bud was steady, ambitious, good-looking, and sober.

The wedding reception was held at the home of Bud's parents. The pictures of Cora's father and mother were featured on the piano. Folks admired them. Cora's father looked dignified and intelligent. Her mother looked stately, though young. The guests were sorry that such fine people hadn't lived long enough to attend their daughter's wedding and see what a good match the girl had made.

But my father puzzled over the pictures for a long time and then he sought out Jonas Hall in the corner where Jonas sat, smiling and nodding. Jonas, being a poet, liked weddings and romance, music and flowers, pageantry and beauty.

"Jonas," said my father, "I've seen Cora's father someplace. I know I have. Do you suppose he ever came through here on business?"

"Bud Growder is a lucky man," said Jonas. "He's marrying a beautiful girl who is also resourceful. She's smart and she's lovely."

"Of course she is. But I was asking you . . . . . ."

"Pretty as they come and smarter than he deserves. She's the answer to a dream, George."

"I agree. But what I was saying, Jonas, is that I do think I've met her father somewhere."

"Of course you've met her father," said Jonas. "You've met him a dozen times, probably. He's only been dead for two months. Her father was Piggy Nelson. He raised hogs out back of Big Brook, where she came from."

"Mrs. Wheeler said she came on the mail stage from Cranston . . . ."

Jonas smiled. "George," he said, "Do you suppose anybody asked the driver where she got on? I don't even care where she came from. I love her. But you asked and I told you. Why do you want to argue about it?"

"I still think you're crazy," said my father. "That picture isn't Piggy Nelson."

"Who said it was? I said her father was Piggy Nelson. That picture is Tennyson at the age of 58. It's out of the *Literary Encyclopedia*. The woman is Elizabeth Barrett Browning. Now stop prying into things, George, and sit down here beside me and we'll enjoy this wonderful festival of young love triumphant."

A man that lives by guile
Suspects guile.
He meets guile with guile;
Ends up on a merry-go-round,
Wondering and worrying
About whether he's chasing or being chased.

—Jonas P. Hall

Chapter IX

Kenny Gage was eight or nine years old when he sent for the radio repair handbook. He couldn't have been over ten because that was the age when Gage ambition started downhill.

As the Gages turned ten, they seemed to receive a sudden revelation of the futility of endeavor. They may have been in telepathic communication with a Biblical prophet. If they were, he was a pessimist. He convinced them that all effort was vain, that glory was a delusion, that the smartest thing they could do was settle for being a Gage. That was an occupation in itself.

Being a Gage meant living in communal happiness with all the other Gages, gardening, hunting, fishing, milking the cow when it was your turn.

The date of ambition loss was as good a way as there was to tell the age of a Gage. They didn't go in for birth certificates. Lily Gage, old Randy's wife, might let a year or so go by before she mentioned to someone that she'd had a baby a while back.

Lily was a confused happy person. Between keeping house and cooking and caring and bearing, she rarely had time to make notes in a family Bible.

It didn't matter, anyway. Nobody really cared how old the Gages were. When they were big enough to look eligible, they voted.

Clint Reynolds, the Cedar River Postmaster, was the first one to find out that ambition still stirred a Gage. Clint found out because he chided Kenny for asking twice in the same day if a package had come for him.

"You know the mail don't come in only once," said Clint. "What are you so eager to get? You think somebody's going to send you a share of the money from Teapot Dome?"

Teapot Dome was one of the big humor subjects for our town. The citizens weren't irate over the villainy involved. They were amused by the trials in which it was proved that Fall had taken the bribe from Doheny that Doheny was proved not to have given to Fall.

But Kenny Gage wasn't interested in Teapot Dome. He said, "There ain't nobody sending me money. They're sending me a book. I'm going to learn how to repair radios and then get a job doing it. Someday I'll be making big money . . . maybe fifty dollars a week."

"A noble dream," said Doc Yates.

Even if all his patients had paid him, a dream more noble than Doc thought Kenny's was, Doc wouldn't have made any fifty dollars a week. Semi-skilled workers were getting thirty-five cents an hour. Henry Ford had startled the industrial world a few years before by giving factory hands five dollars a day.

"Fifty dollars a week," repeated Kenny. "That's what the advertisement said."

"When anybody pays a workingman fifty dollars a week, Kenny," said Clint Reynolds, "the end of the world will be coming close."

But Kenny wasn't listening. He had gone home to wait impatiently for the next morning's mail.

Doc and Clint went on with the bulk mail transaction that Kenny had interrupted. It seemed stupid to both of these men to make the government provide stamps just to be stuck on Doc's bills, cancelled, and then thrown away by the people who got the bills handed to them from the general delivery pigeonholes.

This waste was avoided by an arrangement that involved Clint's putting the bills in the pigeonholes without stamps, in exchange for five cigars. Nobody knew what the government did with the cigars.

On this day, Doc lingered while Clint was pigeonholing.

"Hope Kenny gets his book before the text is outdated," Doc said. "Hope the whole thing isn't a swindle."

"Fifty bucks a week," said Clint, "is a swindle when it's mentioned. But he'll probably get the book. It might be a good book, too. But why don't these outfits make realistic promises about rewards?"

"Because realism doesn't mix with dreams," said Doc. "You've got to promise glory to get either the votes or the pennies of the poor. Would Kenny gamble $2.50 to learn a trade that would let him earn your pittance pay?"

"Maybe not. But why always fifty dollars? It's fifty dollars no matter what they're training you for. You're promised fifty dollars a week if you pay for learning how to raise giant frogs, bronze baby shoes, or sell soap."

Doc shook his head at Clint's lack of understanding.

"It's because they're promoting fantasy," he said. "If they bring common sense into the pitch, they'd puncture the cloud. That would be criminal."

"Criminal the way it is. There should be laws against it. If people can't protect themselves, the government ought to protect them."

"Protect them against dreams?"

"Against swindlers and con men," said Clint.

"Same thing," said Doc. "They sell dreams. Only thing you gotta watch out for when you buy a dream is whether it lasts long enough to be worth the money or whether it's a poor trade."

"Did you ever buy a dream, Doc?"

"Well, I paid to go to medical school. They sold me a dream there of teaching people about sanitation and proper food. I guess that was a fair buy. I still dream about it once in awhile until Mona Harris wakes me up by asking why I don't try giving Annie Trembley distilled June bug juice for her indigestion. I passed up a good dream once, too. A deal on some stock."

"Would you have made a lot of money?"

"No. I told you it was a dream. But it was a year before anybody proved there wasn't any copper or any mine, either. I could have bought hopes for a fortune for that year for only about seventy-five bucks."

Clint pondered on that as he finished sorting the unofficial mail. He didn't see Doc Yates leave. He didn't see Mrs. Peters come in, either. He was wondering where a man should look to find a listing of outfits that sold dreams.

Without raising his head, he said, "Do you suppose I could buy some delusions somewhere for ten dollars?"

There was no answer. Mrs. Peters had spun around and left. She almost ran as she crossed the street to Mrs. Wheeler's house to spread the word that Clint Reynolds, after taking the pledge just the week before, was already looking for a place to buy some whiskey.

The story could end there. It could be only the story of a boy whom two men knew should be either envied or scorned but were not sure which. It could end with Kenny waiting for a book that never came, the advertising being a snare. It could end with education in reality. It could had it taken place in any town but ours.

Cedar River was a town that had always been ruled by the hill gods to whom reality never did have the same appeal as fantasy. The hill gods love to laugh. In Kenny Gage's quest for skills that might lead him on to riches, the hill gods saw their chance. Kenny got his book.

To understand the odds against Kenny's ever learning to

repair radios from a book, a person must remember that radios were not then common, especially in the smaller towns.

Cedar River folks did not yet understand the secret of sound transfer from a groove in a record to a man's ears. They had no more chance of probing the mystery of a radio set than they had of knowing how the vaudeville magician made the lady disappear.

People who visited homes where there were radios kept looking for wires. They refused to believe that a little box could grab sounds that were hovering in the air.

Yet here was a kid, and a Gage kid at that, carrying around a book filled with diagrams, trying to turn himself into some kind of a damn genius. He didn't have a radio, either. All his funds had gone to buy the book which told him how to fix something he didn't even have. How stupid could you get? Pass the beans, Miranda.

Anyone in town who had a radio certainly wasn't going to let Kenny Gage play around with it.

The scoffers forgot Doc Yates. Doc had a radio. He had one of those old "peanut tube" sets, limited in its range but almost impossible to mess up. Actually, all those old sets were limited in range. There was a fairly strong station in Cranston, ten miles downriver, so Cedar River got Cranston weather, Cranston news, a Cranston announcer's choice of music, and descriptions of ball games that came to Cranston by telegraph and then were faked by someone in the studio who pretended that he was at the game.

Clint Reynolds used to fuss because he had to take the Cranston station's editorial views and a Cranston interpretation of world happenings. Doc Yates claimed that this was all for the good.

"Cedar River people get enough bad new," Doc said. "My soul, they make bad news. They certainly don't need to hear about problems in New Jersey or China."

But Doc did like to listen to music from Cranston. He liked the good station recordings of Caruso. Caruso didn't sing as well through Doc's radio as he did in New York City, but even a scratchy Caruso was a pleasant change from Mrs. Trembley's volunteered renditions of old songs.

Doc Yates' big trouble, and he admitted it himself, was that he had humanitarian impulses. He resented them but he was born with them and he couldn't seem to stifle them. He'd make up his mind to pin a blast on Jeb Seekings the next time Jeb told him he had indigestion and didn't know why, but then he'd find himself trying to ease Jeb's pain without more than a little growling.

Doc didn't want to be guilty of helping mankind in its constant stupid blunders. Still he helped. He even found himself wanting to help Kenny Gage, as Kenny plugged along with the radio book, drawing charts and pretending that tangles of hay wire were induction coils and being frustrated by not having something to tear apart and put together again.

So Doc pulled two wires loose in his radio one day and then sent for Kenny Gage. Kenny took the radio home, got out his book, and went to work.

Kenny's tool kit was about what anyone would expect a Gage to have. He had some fence pliers, a couple of bent screwdrivers, a pruning knife, and a roll of tape.

The Gages were salvagers. They had odds and ends of junk all over the place, car engine parts, clock parts, gun parts, and separator parts. Kenny had to push a lot of stuff to one side of the workbench, not all of it but enough to give him elbow room.

All evening, with a short pause for supper, Kenny kept plugging away. He had been too eager, naturally, to get right into the heart of that radio to notice the loose wires. He loosened lots of wires, anyway, but he crimped them back together where they seemed to match.

About midnight, he had everything back in place. He'd found a couple of things he didn't remember taking out, but one fitted nicely under a tube and one went into a slot in a spindle. The book didn't show those but he thought they'd been covered by some wires that he'd led around in a different place.

When he turned the radio on, it worked. It worked well. Before school in the morning he rushed it to Doc Yates' house. Doc snapped the switch. The result startled him. Intead of normal scratchy sounds, there were clear tones and mellow voices.

Doc twisted the dial. There was music that sounded as though it were in the next room. With another twist there came a weather report from Poughkeepsie, New York.

"Is it O.K. Doc?" asked Kenny.

Doc scowled. "Can't tell much yet," he said. "Have to wait until tonight. Radio is always better at night."

But Doc didn't wait that long. He rushed through his morning calls. He was brusque with Mrs. Turner when she came for his afternoon office hours. He locked up before three o'clock.

Back in his study with that radio, he went from one station to another, listening to announcers in Montana, Texas, and Iowa. When he finally got a program from London, he shut off the set and went looking for Kenny, taking the radio with him.

Kenny had stopped in at the garage to talk with Bullnose Perkins. Doc cleared a place on Bullnose's bench. "Listen to this," he said. "You and I are going to make a million dollars."

He turned the dial. There was a snap, a curl of smoke, a small explosion, then wild flames. Bullnose grabbed a welding glove, snatched up the radio, hurled it through the window. It landed smack in a pail half-filled with gasoline that Bullnose had set outside after cleaning some engine parts.

The fire was contained but fierce. All that was left was a mess of melted dials, twisted bits of metal, shriveled wires.

"Can you remember what in hell you did?" roared Doc.

"Well," said Kenny. "Well . . . ."

Calming, Doc shrugged. "Never mind," he said. "I guess it's just as well. Cedar River isn't ready yet for full contact with the world."

Dedicated women could be sent by God.
That's what the speaker at Chataqua said.
He said they cleanse the souls of men;
Lift their hearts and make them pure.
Snatch them from the Devil's grasp;
Turn them toward salvation.

No doubt a man in trouble needs
That kind of help to cleanse and lift,
To snatch and turn.
But if he's doing all right by himself,
A dedicated woman is a nuisance.
She supplies the trouble
She resents not being there.

—Jonas P. Hall

Chapter X

Mrs. Kelly filled the heads of the Cedar River youngsters with more random knowledge than would be spouted by an encyclopedia editor under a hypnotic compulsion to babble. To her scholars, she set extreme goals of learning.

American history was one of her points of particular concentration. Her idea of a good citizen was one who could recite the Declaration of Independence, the Constitution, Lincoln's Gettysburg Address, and the names of all the Presidents, without pausing for more than five deep breaths.

She said, "In order to understand what motivated great men in their heroic deeds, you have to study their lives and pick up clues that may guide your own conduct."

We were regularly assigned men to study and report on. One week, I drew Ethan Allen.

I rather liked Ethan. He seemed rough and rustic as though he might have fitted perfectly into the casual life of our town. I could imagine him drinking and laughing with my uncle

Oscar, shocking Mrs. Wheeler, tramping in the woods with the boisterous older Gages.

As I read more and more about Ethan Allen, I became more and more enthused about him. But then, I found a statement that reminded me of someone I wasn't enthused about at all.

"My goodness," I said to my father. "That sounds exactly like Florence Coosterman."

"What does?" asked my father.

"Something Ethan Allen said."

"Florence," said my father, "is ahead of Ethan Allen by the length of a sap trail. How did you manage to put her in his class?"

"He said if he were defeated in battle, he'd retire to the mountains and wage war against human nature at large."

"Quite an ambitious campaign."

"Well, that's what Florence Coosterman does," I said. "She wages war against human nature at large."

My father shook his head. "From all you've told me," he said, "she doesn't do any such thing. Florence wages war against people and their human nature is her ally in the fight."

I thought about that and decided he was right. Florence did use other people's weaknesses. She studied their emotions and baited her traps with phantom solutions to their problems.

She was mature enough to take advantage of the rapid emotional changes that the rest of us went through and she didn't. Most grade school youngsters can go from friendship to enmity or enmity to friendship overnight. Florence's enmity was constant.

While we could greet each other in the morning with complete forgetfulness of harsh words spoken the day before, Florence never forgot anything, never forgave anything, held steady in her drive to prove herself superior to us all.

She took advantage of our desire to believe that nobody could be as objectionable as we were often tempted to think she was. When she bit us, we bandaged the wound, forgot it, held out the hand of friendship again. At that point, Florence bit us harder.

She was dangerous even in the spring, when Cedar River was a storybook delight with the ice floating down the river and the south wind expanding the air as winter pressures lifted.

Inside the schoolhouse, of course, spring was a little less enjoyable. Mrs. Kelly permitted the opening of windows only when our suffering became acute or her own became unbearable. Open windows let in outdoor noises and thus ruined the figuratively academic atmosphere.

The physical atmosphere was ruined from inside. The best adjective for spring-warmed indoor air is "robust." If there were fifteen scholars, at least three of them had been sewed up in their underwear since October and all fifteen had been put on a sulphur and molasses schedule the morning of the first day that the temperature went above forty degrees.

We always had spring fever in the schoolhouse, too. It came over us and it did strange things to our metabolism and our mental alertness. It made us dream and forget things and stare at our books without seeing them. It was powerful. It was painful, too.

Mrs. Kelly didn't believe in spring fever. She called us lazy or inattentive or stupid or insolent. It didn't matter what descriptive word she chose. The punishment was the same except that there were two extra wallops for insolence, but they came after the victim was numb so they were wasted except for their temporary effect on the rest of the school.

The year that I was in the fifth grade I seemed to suffer more than I had ever suffered before from this spring hypnosis. I needed to get out of school and walk on unrestricted paths and watch the resurgence of growth.

But Washington's Birthday was past and both Easter vacation and Patriot's Day were a month's maulings away. I could see no escape from stuffy books. That was why I was so completely startled when Florence Coosterman spoke her words of joy.

She winked at me in the schoolyard at recess time. She whispered in conspiratorial tones.

"Three days until our holiday," she said.

"Holiday?" I said. "When's there a holiday?"

"Our special one for . . . Oh, I was thinking you were a member. I guess you're not . . ."

"Member of what?" I demanded

"I can't tell you, she said. "It's a secret."

The bell rang. We went inside. It was a long afternoon. No boy wants to be left out of a secret society, especially one that has its own holidays. After school I grabbed Florence.

"Listen, " I said, "what do you have to do to be a member of whatever club gets a special holiday? Tell me. I won't say anything to anybody else."

Her answer was typical of Florence. "What will you give me if I let you join?" she asked. "Everybody can choose a new member each spring. I'd choose you if you gave me that wooden chain you carved."

The chain was a big sacrifice, but the club and the holiday seemed worth it. I reached inside my shirt and gave her the chain, four pine links representing effort and some blood.

"All right," said Florence. "Now, remember, it's a secret. You don't tell in school and you don't tell at home. The geese come back north on the sixteenth of March. That's the holiday."

"A holiday because geese come back?"

"If you're a member of the goose club, it is. Geese are a part of precious wildlife, so every member of the goose club gets a whole morning off to watch them or think about them or anything else. It's a special holiday for goose clubbers. Remember I was absent last year . . . all morning?"

I didn't remember at all, but I nodded. Florence gave me further instructions and made me swear a terrible oath of silence. I felt like a secret prince for the next three days.

On March sixteenth, I felt like an emperor. I wandered down to the Rock River Flow and threw stones in the open water. I sat on a big boulder and dreamed of summer coming. I skipped and shouted and tried to merge with spring.

I didn't see any geese, but I shared my lunch with an early ranging chipmunk.

Noon hour ended too soon. I joined the group entering the schoolhouse. I hated to go back, but at least I knew the code words that would make Mrs. Kelly smile and approve of my morning's excursion into spring. Florence had told me just what to say. The phrase was on my lips as I answered my summons to come to the front of the room.

"Where were you this morning?" asked Mrs. Kelly.

I leaned over toward her and smiled broadly.

"Ho-o-onk," I said.

She looked puzzled. "Honk?" she said.

"I'm a new goose clubber," I whispered.

She stared. "You're a what?" she shouted.

I started to lean again. Then I was caught in a prickly wave of horror as I suddenly knew. I knew. My legs became boneless things which threatened to sag and let me slump. I stole a look past my right shoulder to the front seat where Florence had a handkerchief stuffed in her mouth, her face red from stifling laughter.

Then I gulped and waited silently, realizing that I wasn't a goose clubber at all, not at all.

I was just a goose, a gone goose, about to be clubbed.

Hunting's not a sport in this town.
It's part of living.
It's an understood duty to home and family.

These men will tell you
They don't hunt so they can see
Fluid grace stopped in motion.
They don't want to kill
So they can smell death.
They're just doing some trading
At nature's bargain counter,
Getting economic benefits
For the price of a cartridge.

Years ago, the Romans did their business even cheaper.
They used the same sword
On eight or ten Helvetians.

—Jonas P. Hall

Chapter XI

An observer might have called it a coincidence and a historian might have called it a tradition. Actually it was planned as a defensive preparation.

The Cedar River men gathered at Turner's store, on the night before hunting season officially opened, in order that each one might buy some little thing which he could say he'd been clean out of for a year.

Except for a few deviationists who secretly thought they were deep thinkers and so bought compasses or new knives, the men bought cartridges. They bought them casually, as though someone else's purchase had reminded them of their own need.

They said, "Well . . . I might give it a try in the morning, too, and I know I ain't got a bullet in the house because I was looking for one when the fox came through the field last spring."

They said, 'Golly, now that I think of it, I've got everything else ready to go hunting and I haven't got a shell . . . not a one. After all, there ain't been no need since last fall."

A stranger who overheard the remarks in Turner's store on the night before deer season would have thought that the whole town was completely defenseless from the end of the season until the start of the next. That was the impression intended.

Actually, not only did every man present have a deer hanging up somewhere, but a group decision had already been made as to whose turn it was to bring his quarry into town first to have the deer tagged and to get his picture taken by the reporter from the *Cranston Gazette* who was always waiting.

Doc Yates, a friend of the *Cranston* editor, had come back to Cedar River, once, chuckling about an innocent reporter who had questioned the positiveness of getting a picture.

"A man might hang around all day and just waste his time," the reporter had said.

"The man hadn't better," the editor told him. "The man had better be there at nine o'clock, on the button, and be back here with his picture by ten."

"How do you know . . . . .?"

"Oh, shut up," had been the answer. "Look, I've lost track, but I think it's Reggie Gage or Jeb Seekings that's due. If it's Jeb . . . well, his features are disorganized, you might say, so you take a side view. If it's Reggie Gage, for God's sake don't let him wear that safety contest medal he traded the Boy Scout out of. Last time we showed him with that medal we had fourteen letters of protest, from the American Legion to the Temperance League, all denying that Reggie's medal was anything that reflected discredit on them."

Jubal Dean, the game warden, knew what the situation was, just as the editor did. But Jubal never tried to interfere with the first day presentation of deer at the tagging station.

Jubal might have been able to prove, had he tried, that even though the hunter had witnesses to the fact that he'd just bought his bullets the night before, two-hour-old deer weren't dark and dried out around the dressing cut. But Jubal didn't try to prove anything at all.

Jubal operated within the limits of the Cedar River code, which stated that it was unfair of him to make any accusations until he'd warned the suspect three times in advance, checked to see if meat was lacking in the family larder, and then caught the violator in the act of shooting.

So, every year, Cedar River carried out this little drama of the late purchase of bullets, the alternating honor of being first, and the guarantee to a reporter of a picture at nine o'clock. It was as rigid as the dutiful drinking sessions on New Year's Eve.

Only once was there a serious attempt at protest or prosecution. The protest wasn't made to Jubal Dean. It was made to Jesse Hill, the town policeman, by a salesman who had tried to make a few fast dollars.

"I've been cheated," said the salesman to Jesse. "I guess the charge would be conspiracy to defraud."

"Who conspired against you" asked Jesse.

"The whole damned town, I think."

"You'll have to be more definite than that," said Jesse. "I can't arrest the whole town and bring business and production to a halt. Besides, we only got two cells."

"Well," said the salesman, "it was on account of a little innocent thing that I thought of in the store last night. The place was full of fellows buying bullets . . ."

"I'll bet it was."

"So, what the hell . . . a little flutter . . . that's all right, isn't it? I said that if anybody in that gang wanted to guess the weight and the sex of the first deer tagged, I'd pay two to one, on dollar bets . . . if the sex was right and the weight was within five pounds."

"Giving them the short end, wasn't you?" asked Jesse. "Seems as though the odds on a guess like that ought to be closer to five hundred to one."

"Of course they are," said the salesman. "That's why I figured I'd . . . well, that isn't the point. The point is that fifteen men bet with me and every one of them won. There's something funny there."

"Might be, at that."

"You ought to do something about it, then."

"I will," said Jesse. "It's too late now, but you come back next year and make the same offer. Notify me when you do."

"You going to set a trap for them?" asked the salesman.

Jesse smiled. "Jesus no," he said. "I'm going to get a bet down with you, myself."

First he had them scratching heads.
They scratched because they didn't know
Why Oscar should be interested in soil.
He never farmed.
He never gardened.
But still, they thought his interest was good,
Until they discovered the reason for it.

Good soil grows better fruit.
Better fruit makes better wine.
Oscar didn't care who grew the fruit
If he could harvest it.

They found that out.
Then they said that Oscar's interest in soil
Was selfish, therefore bad.

I'd give up on people
If there were anything more challenging to watch.
How can building soil be an evil thing
Just because Oscar is a drunk?

—*Jonas P. Hall*

Chapter XII

My Uncle Oscar loved the things that grew from the soil. He picked the pin cherries carefully in clusters and his touch was tender as he took the berries from the bush. When he gathered violets, he was as careful of the stems as of the blooms.

He put all these beautiful things in crocks and covered them lovingly with sugar and yeast and water. He was possibly more appreciative of what nature provided than was any other man in Cedar River. He knew there was a potential key to paradise in everything that bloomed.

Nature rewarded Oscar for his devotion. She worked in a mellow manner on the substance in his crocks, performing feats of alchemy that converted even the humble dandelions and tender black birch twigs into fluids that brightened the sun and brought the stars closer to the evening river.

On a bushel of arbutus blooms that Uncle Oscar set to brewing one spring, nature did such a superb job that when Oscar was induced by promoters of civic betterment to part with a gallon of the blessed beverage for a town treat, the entire population walked in the mist with the muses and everyone spoke in iambic pentameter for a week.

Occasionally Oscar was driven by economic need to produce beverages for the market, but at those times he made no pretense of artistry. He worked with a fierce savagery akin to that of an artist who hires out to paint a barn.

He didn't use the harvest of groves or gardens in his commercial ventures. He threw garbage and grain and molasses and yeast into tubs to ferment and then distilled the horrible result. He put this into syrup tins and rushed downriver to sell it before it dissolved the containers. He resented the whole deal.

Fortunately, Oscar's financial pressures were few. He could end most of them by gentle swindles or by borrowings from the innocent. He also got a little cash from the sale of his blissful, lovingly concocted brews to a selected customer list.

It was for the sake of these customers, he claimed, as well as to keep his own soul pure, that he was constantly pleading for the preservation of humus and the plowing in of organic substances. He wanted the earth to retain its richness.

He said, "All you farmers are trustees of the soil. You ought to be ashamed of abusing it."

He scolded Deak Trembley in public for growing small fruits that were less than perfect. "You ain't mulched your raspberries in three years," he told Deak. "You ain't trimmed your grapes, neither."

"Why should I?" asked Deak. "Somebody always steals them just when they're hitting the peak of ripeness."

"That's a selfish way to talk," said Oscar. "Some poor guy works hard in the night to gather them and he's got a right to expect them to be juicy, not small and shameful."

Deak questioned this philosophy. He denied his responsibility to crooks. So Oscar had to put up with Deak's selfishness, or at least he chose to for the sake of keeping Deak from getting too solidly founded suspicions about what was happening to his grapes. It was probably for the same reason that Oscar kept Deak on the small beverage customer list.

Deak appreciated being one of Oscar's selections for surplus buying. He even defied his wife when she tried to end his favored relationship with the master distiller and blender.

Except for a bit of dutiful nagging, Annie Trembley was tolerant of Deak's activities. She had never been a masterful woman. But after Deak got himself saved at a revival meeting one year, she developed the absurd idea that he should stay saved.

She figured he might have a chance if he stayed away from the Devil's recruiting agents, particularly Uncle Oscar. Deak protested this notion.

"It ain't that I'm a bosom pal of Oscar's," said Deak. "It's just that I like to do a little trading with him, here and there, for this and that."

"Oscar only trades in one thing," said Annie. "His trading is immoral and illegal and he cheats you anyway."

Deak didn't mind being accused of breaking moral or statutory laws. He hated to be hailed as a poor trader, though.

"I get my money's worth," he said. "What's a few dollars compared with a fresh outlook on problems?"

"You can get a fresh outlook any Sunday in church," said Annie.

That appeal failing, Annie's next step was to try to stop the traffic from the other end. She caught Oscar in the store and explained that she didn't want to have Deak refueled for flying.

"Deak doesn't need any help from your vile bottles," she said. "Deak can get all the help he needs from a better source."

Uncle Oscar was puzzled. In the first place, he rarely had bottles. For his prime stock he used jugs and fruit jars. In the second place, he hadn't heard about any competition.

"What better source?" he asked Annie. "Who else around here is making liquor?"

"I mean," said Annie, "that when Deak feels downcast or tested beyond his strength, he can get help from heaven."

"Heaven is helping Deak?"

GENERAL STO

"Both of us. We've both put ourselves in heaven's hands. If we're in trouble or need anything, heaven will send help."

Oscar didn't argue. He wasn't in a position to check Annie's statement with her announced benefactor. So Annie took her store purchases and started for the door. A wandering dog got tangled in her feet. Down she went.

She clung tightly to both bags as she fell. But she found herself unable to rise with both arms thus engaged. "Don't just stand there," she said to Oscar. "I need some help."

"From me?" asked Uncle Oscar. "Gosh, you just said you'd be getting it from heaven."

The loungers roared but Annie wasn't bested.

"I would be," she said, "except that the good Lord certainly isn't going to work any miracles while the Devil has a spy around to watch how he does it."

Thus outworded by a woman, Uncle Oscar's dignity demanded that he avoid future encounters with her. He dropped Deak from his sales list, shaking his head firmly when approached with a plea.

"I ain't selling to nobody that don't manure his crops," said Oscar. "You fit so good with heaven, let it rain you some communion wine."

According to Reverend Adams,
God appreciated Job's devotion.
God loved him.
But Job stook out.
He was visible,
So he was smitten.

Reverend Adams didn't answer me
When I asked,
"In that case, might it be better
To spend each Sunday
Hidden in a hay mow
Than in a high pulpit preaching?"

—Jonas P. Hall

Chapter XIII

Squirrel Jordan's real name was Galahad. His mother knew better than to expect Cedar River to use a name like that, but she couldn't resist attaching it to him. His family called him Laddie, but when he started school he became known as Gal.

In the fourth grade, this nickname tempted Ned Trembley to draw some oral conclusions about Gal's manhood. That was a mistake. Gal showed Ned that silence is wisdom when the opposition hasn't been tested. Then he announced that he wasn't going to be called Gal any more.

He didn't tell us what to call him, though, so we worked around the difficulty by pointing and saying, "Hey,"

Then, when he was eleven years old, he discovered a jug of my Uncle Oscar's ambrosia tucked under the floor joists of the town hall during a square dance. He choked down enough of it to stimulate him into climbing a tree and chirping at the moon.

After that he didn't have a chance in the world of being

called anything else but Squirrel. He didn't mind that name anyway. He probably recognized its poetic justice and its applicability.

When he was twelve years old, he became an atheist. That wasn't a result of study or soul searching. It was brought on by pressure from a member of the guild of the pious, aided by Squirrel's own strong belief in the infallible power of the commonly accepted Deity. He believed himself into disbelief.

A few of the boys were fishing one day down by the Rock River Flow. Among the group was Pete Baker. Pete was a repulsively righteous specimen whose parents promoted togetherness by forcing each member of the family to recite a Bible verse every morning at the breakfast table. They stimulated sanctimoniousness by giving lurid descriptions at bedtime of the horrors of Hell and the ease of entry to that place.

Pete Baker didn't like Squirrel Jordan. He was afraid of him. He knew that Squirrel was a doomed sinner because of that whiskey-drinking, tree-climbing episode, and he also knew that it wasn't healthy to stay close to sinners because the Lord might pick any moment to smite them.

Pete thought that it was as daring to hang around Squirrel Jordan as it would have been to make a practice of holding one's head six inches from the target on a rifle range.

Down on the Rock River Flow, during that fishing excursion, the clouds started to gather and the thunder rolled in from the west. The rain massed on the ridges and started toward the valley in a sheet, blotting out the sky and the trees.

The boys crawled into a dense cluster of small spruces, intertwined and matted in a manner impenetrable to weather. As they squirmed under this shelter, somebody stepped on Squirrel Jordan's hand and Squirrel swore. He swore capably.

"There," said Pete Baker, "that's probably the last straw. I'm going around on the other side of this tangle. When the thunderbolt strikes Squirrel, I don't want to get hit."

The lightning was close and the sky took on a weired light. The wind was whipping the crested pines and the hemlocks were creaking as they were forced to yield some of their stubborn rigidity. The boys were swayed by the arguments of Pete Baker. They started to follow him.

Then a streak of lightning did blast down at the edge of the flow. It didn't hit Squirrel Jordan, though. It hit a lonesome maple, blew a chunk right out of it, and threw the chunk fifty feet in a whizzing trajectory through the spruces to hit Pete Baker a glancing wallop that knocked him cold.

This experience proved something to Squirrel Jordan. He couldn't believe that God would use his own champion for target practice. But he couldn't believe, either, that God could be a poor shot. The God of the Cedar River Christians was just and infallible. Clipping Pete Baker didn't make any sense.

There was only one answer. Squirrel concluded that there was no God. He stopped believing. Upon such incidents are philosophies molded and souls lost.

Squirrel Jordan didn't particularly want to convert anyone else to his atheism, but he realized that there was some publicity value in his non-belief and as long as he was going to challenge the existence of God he might as well impress someone with his daring.

After all, if he was wrong he was going to roast in Hell, so a little preliminary admiration of his boldness was due him.

He approached me at recess. "I'm an atheist," he mumbled.

I was a Henley man right then, full of admiration for "Invictus," I was worshipping "whatever gods may be," and I was engaged in creating those gods and assigning to them the characteristics that proper gods should have. I didn't want to give them up.

Besides that, I was afraid of outright atheism. I had heard that there would be a high price paid in the hereafter for unbelief.

"Do you want to be an atheist, too?" asked Squirrel.

"No," I said. "Atheism is unbelief and unbelief has a high price."

He thought that over. "How high?" he asked.

"I don't know, but I think it's higher than I want to pay. Why don't you be a pagan like me? I think that's cheaper."

He seemed to be tempted by this possible bargain in the defiance of orthodoxy, but he finally shook his head.

"Nope," he said. "I'm an atheist."

He looked around for someone else to shock and he spotted Florence Coosterman, standing alone in her usual self-sufficiency, pining, probably, for the days when the Aztecs tore beating hearts from living victims and ate them raw.

Squirrel tapped Florence on the shoulder. "I'm an atheist," he said. "I don't believe in God."

"Don't be silly," said Florence. "Look, can you crack your knuckles? I can."

If Voltaire had met with that kind of a reception, his whole life might have been changed. But Squirrel tried again.

"I guess I'll go to Hell," he said, "for denying God."

"Probably will," said Florence.

"Don't you *care*?"

"Well," she said, "there's one thing. . .those glass alleys your aunt brought you from Atlantic City. . .they'll melt down in Hell from the heat. Now marbles would bake harder because they're clay. I'll trade you a marble for every five alleys you've got."

"You crazy or something?" asked Squirrel. "I only got ten of those alleys and I'm not going to trade them for two marbles."

"You have ten alleys?" asked Florence. "That's funny. That's a real coincidence. That's exactly the number I need to keep me from telling Mrs. Kelly that you're an atheist."

Horror hit Squirrel Jordan. A future God was one thing to contemplate facing but an immediate Mrs. Kelly was another.

"You wouldn't tell Mrs. Kelly," said Squirrel.

"I wouldn't want to," said Florence, "but my conscience would make me unless I could bribe it not to. Ten alleys would do the trick. What about it, Squirrel? You better hurry. My conscience is eager."

The bell was ringing when Squirrel rejoined me.

"Tell me about this pagan deal," he said. "I changed my mind. I'm not going to be an atheist. You were right. The price is awful high."

"It's only a matter of time,"
Said Doc Yates,
"Before the subsidizers of the unfit
Become too unfit to subsidize them."

Everybody thought that was funny,
Except Deak Trembley.
Deak went home and worried for three days
About which side to join.

—*Jonas P. Hall*

Chapter XIV

Freddie Grouper had trouble coping with life. He found most of the activities of the solid citizens too complex. He could learn rules but he couldn't apply them sensibly.

Like the rest of Mrs. Kelly's scholars, Freddie learned many maxims as a part of the Kelly enrichment program. He knew most of "Poor Richard's Almanac," and he could quote from Elbert Hubbard.

Mrs. Kelly held Cedar River schoolboys to the belief that hard work settles all problems, that honesty is the best policy, and that anyone can rise in the world if he does each job to the best of his ability.

"Don't ever admit that you can't do something," Mrs. Kelly said. "You can try it, anyway. You might surprise yourself."

"When someone hires you to work," she said, "work like a person who is eager. Take hold and make an impression."

Freddie Grouper listened to all these little lectures, most of which were given as vocal accompaniment to wallopings. He took the words literally and he tried to apply them to the jobs he got.

Mr. Turner was one employer who suffered. He offered Freddie a quarter to help unload a shipment of goods for the grocery store. Freddie grabbed hold of a barrel of molasses.

"Wait a minute," said Mr. Turner. "You need a hand with that. It weighs a . . . ."

He was too late. Freddie had committed himself to lifting the barrel from the wagon bed. The barrel had slipped, despite his determination. The angle of fall was just right to spring the hoops and the staves. Wide gaps opened.

"Golly," said Freddie. "There sure was a lot of molasses in that barrel, wasn't there?"

"You haven't got a brain in your thick head," said Mr. Turner. "You walrus-witted . . . you eager clown . . . ."

"Mrs. Kelly told us to be eager," said Freddie. "She said if we were eager, we'd make an impression."

Mr. Turner's answer came close to heresy. "Mrs. Kelly can be wrong, " he said. "This time, she is."

The growing circle of spilled molasses observers shook their heads. They thought Mrs. Kelly was right. Freddie had made an impression on them. He'd made a definite impression. He'd proved that he couldn't be trusted to use common sense.

The townspeople were glad that they had received this impression without having to pay for the damage done. They were sorry that Mr. Turner had to pay, but better him than them.

Only one man did more than watch the results of Freddie's indoctrinated eagerness. My Uncle Oscar was down on his hands and knees, capitalizing on the Turner misfortune.

The storekeeper yelled at Uncle Oscar.

"What do you think you're doing?" he shouted.

"Just scraping up some of this wasting molasses," said the gleaner. "I might find a poor family that needs it."

"Where'd you get the dustpan and the buckets so fast?"

Uncle Oscar grinned. "By being eager," he said. "By following Mrs. Kelly's good advice."

TURNE

"That's my molasses," said Mr. Turner.

"It's no good to you. If you saved one cupful, nobody in town would buy molasses from you for the next ten years, for fear of getting poisoned. Ain't that right?"

Victimized by clumsiness, taunted by valid philosophy, Mr. Turner became unreasonable. He knew very well, of course, why Uncle Oscar wasn't afraid of being poisoned. When Uncle Oscar was finished with the molasses, its product would be antiseptic. Molasses plus yeast yields rum.

"Get away from my molasses," roared Mr. Turner. "I don't care if it all sinks down into the gravel. You can't have it. I'd rather see it lost than give it to you . . . ."

"I never heard of such inhumanity," said a shocked voice.

Mr. Turner looked up. A stylishly dressed woman was standing by a big car. She was peering through the group, looking sympathetically at Uncle Oscar. "You poor man," she said.

"Yes, ma'am," said Uncle Oscar. "I ain't had no job for five years. I need this molasses here."

"Oh, my soul," said Mr. Turner. He spun around and left.

"Come on," said the lady. "You don't need to scrape up that dirty stuff to feed your family. Here . . . take this . . . ."

Uncle Oscar's hand closed on a bill.

"Thank you, ma'am," he said, "Thank you."

"That's all right," she said, "I was going to buy a few things in this store but I certainly wouldn't patronize anyone who lacks every element of charitable feeling."

"No, ma'am, said Uncle Oscar, "I don't blame you."

The car drove off. Uncle Oscar peeked at his palm. "Twenty bucks," he said. He looked at Freddie Grouper, standing dumbly in confusion.

"You keep on being eager," said Uncle Oscar. "Forget what Turner said. Mrs. Kelly is the one to believe. Eagerness pays off."

"What you men have to remember,"
Said Deak Trembley,
"Is that a sex that defied God
Just to taste a Northern Spy
Is capable of even stranger sins."

Jeb Seekings disagreed.
He said it was a Baldwin.

— *Jonas P. Hall*

Chapter XV

Clem Woolcott was tall and he was tough. He was a white water man and a dark rum drinker. He could take a bateau through a hollow log. He could pry loose the key and then jump over the breaking jam. He could knock down a moose with his fist.

Clem was a rough fighting some a woods god and a tree nymph. He had a jagged smile that would cut a cloud in half and let the sun shine through. He had a scowl that would reach into the black heart of a crooked bartender and short-circuit his pocket picking hands.

Clem was a hero to every boy in Cedar River, but no boy wanted to draw his name when Ben McCord, the master driver, put the spy slips in the hat. Clem was too hard to keep track of.

The spy slips were assignments in an information service. When the crews left the winter woods, there was always a break of maybe two or three weeks before the drive started. The men drew their pay and scattered. Some went home.

Some hung around our town. But some lost track of distance in their pursuit of delights.

A drive crew could always be assembled but there were certain specialists who were worth making an effort to find. These were boatmen or old hands that knew the eddies or experts with wing booms or straw bosses who could spot little jams before they turned into big ones.

The ideal way to control these men and still give them some pre-drive freedom would have been to loop long lines around their necks, let them roam, and then bring them to a landing with a windlass when they were wanted. That method wasn't practical, so Ben McCord hired boys as informers.

The boys weren't expected to shadow their men. The fifty cent fee was earned by questioning traveling salesmen, by keeping alert to details of fights or poker games, and by trading tips with other boys. Most of the men had patterns of activity. They went to some boarding house, probably no further away than Cranston, and then "did the town" until their money ran out.

When the master driver was ready for his crew, the boys could usually say something like, "Tom Pease is staying at the Crescent and he's been doing his drinking at Farrell's."

That was good enough. Ben McCord could take it from there.

Clem Woolcott, though, was a restless traveler. He was a seeker of entertainment. He was a threat to a boy's future because if a boy were too often wildly wrong then Ben McCord wouldn't hire him the next year.

Besides that, a boy couldn't hope for the bonus if he drew Clem in the lottery. The bonus was a dollar. It went to any boy whose man was physically fit and sober when the master driver grabbed him. Nobody had ever won the bonus but - everybody hoped to.

When I drew Clem Woolcott's name in the lottery, the year I was thirteen, I said a few words that would have brought me a yellow soap mouthwash had I said them at home. My bonus chance was gone. All I could hope for was reasonably accurate location and I had no real confidence in that.

"What's the matter?" asked Ned Trembley. "You get Clem?"

"Yeah," I said. "He's murder. Who'd you get?"

"Lem Sanders," said Bobby. "I almost won with him two years ago. They put him in jail in Cranston on his first night out of the woods. If the river had started to break before his time was up, I'd have had the bonus, but he had another night on the town. When they grabbed him they had to soak him in a spring overnight so he'd know the difference between a peavey and a pine tree."

"Well," I said, "I'll just have to do the best I can."

But I didn't have to do anything at all to begin with. Clem Woolcott was sitting on the store steps waiting for the stage to load the afternoon mail when Agnes Standish tripped over his feet and spilled her groceries. He gathered them up, apologized, got a smile that would have warmed a pail of ice cold milk in five seconds, and offered to help her get her groceries home.

At the Standish farm, Clem was duly invited by Agnes' folks to stay to supper. He said he'd be proud to.

Three days later, Clem was still out there at the Standish's, helping old Bob with the chores, splitting the kindling, fitting the winter cut firewood, sitting in the parlor with Agnes every evening. He seemed to be living contentedly on a plateau.

But I wasn't. I was on a mental roller coaster. I knew Clem's domesticity couldn't last. I hoped it would. I knew it couldn't. Every time Clem came to town with Agnes, I figured that was it. I was sure he'd get on the stage. But he always waited, loaded groceries, went back to the farm.

The wind came from the south. The snow softened. Ben McCord came looking from Clem. I made my report.

"Ride out there with me while I get him," said Ben. "This I gotta see."

He not only saw. He heard. What he heard, he didn't like.

"Yeah," said Clem. "I'm going to marry Agnes here. She agreed to it as soon as I said I'd quit the river."

"You promised *what*?" yelled McCord.

"Promised I'd quit the woods and the river. I'm going to go in with her brother and buy the feed store. We got it all fixed up at the bank."

Ben McCord argued. He argued for an hour. He hated to lose a riverman like Clem Woolcott. He hated to see a pure giant of a white water man, a boatman and a jam breaker and a sluice rider, settle in behind the counter of a feed store and measure out rations for cows.

He hated to see a good log driver quit before he was even halfway stove up; while he still had all his fingers and feet and didn't even walk with a limp.

But Clem was stubborn. He kept shaking his head. Finally, Ben McCord gave up. We started back to town and he mourned at me all the way.

"There you see the power of a good woman," he said. "There you see the call of a clean house and dry sheets and home-made pie and sweet words in the lamplight."

"Yeah," I said.

"Those are wonderful things," he said. "They take a man and smooth off his rough edges and make him a loving husband. They fill his soul with the smell of eternal satisfaction. Remember that."

"I will," I promised.

"And remember, if you ever see one of those women in the distance or even suspect that she's around a bend in the road, run like hell," he said. "A warm house and a soft bed have been the ruination of more good loggers than drink or battle or dull boot caulks."

When we pulled up by Turner's store, Ben said, "I suppose you want your fifty cents."

"What about the bonus?" I asked.

"The bonus? You expect the bonus for Clem?"

"Gosh, Mr. McCord, he was sober, wasn't he? He was fit to work. That's all you ever said about the bonus. You never said anything about not being about to get married."

"Last damn thing I would have though of," he admitted.

"Fit and sober," I said. "And Clem was both."

"All right," said Ben McCord. "Here's your money. But the way I feel right now I'd give you twice as much if he was dirtier than a bog penned pig and drunker than a moonlight fiddler. I'd give you five bucks if he was so stiff I had to roll him to camp with a peavey."

He let me out and drove away.

The next year, though, the terms on the bonus were changed. Ben made the new offer slowly and plainly.

"A dollar extra to any boy," he said, "whose man is fit to work, completely sober, and absolutely uninterested in women of any age or description."

Nobody hoped for bonus money after that. None of us believed in miracles.

A romance can start with a kiss
Or with a battle.
How it begins is not important.
Neither is how it ends.
What's important is that it's romance.
It's rainbow music.
It's singing flowers.
It's a happy thing to have in town.

— Jonas P. Hall

Chapter XVI

Fog and mist alternated with rain. The grass growth resembled that of the old vaudeville magician's magic flower.

The woman's spirits seemed dampened, too. There was a lethargy in her voice. The eye sparkle to which she had clung so long through so many things had given way to a softness which was still a remnant of loveliness but which denied a place to laughter.

"Do you remember Ulysses?" she asked. "Was it Bloom who said that a shout in the street was God?"

It was Jonas Hall she was talking to and Jonas had long been convinced that everything or nothing was God even though the choice of alternatives was confused by a tangle of conflicting evidence.

He shook his head.

"All I know about God, Maurinne," he said, "is that I wish the preachers would tell people that he's either in their hearts or he isn't. I get fed up with descriptions of him floating around to spy on sinners so he can justify sending them to Hell. As far as James Joyce is concerned, I stopped reading his book when he told me about the sun setting behind the town hall that faced south. To deny God and turn around and accuse him of making the sun set in the north on some day that Joyce decided he did it . . . well, that was enough for me."

"You're too practical," she said.

That might have been the first time in sixty years that anyone had called Jonas Hall practical. He had to stop to decide whether Maurinne Hodges was losing her mind or he was getting hard of hearing.

"Why are we talking about James Joyce, anyway?" he asked. "Why have we moved a Dublin Irishman into these hills with his dour moods and his dull vision and his language that storms through the thick brush instead of following a clear trail?"

Maurinne laughed. "You were the one who stopped me to talk," she said. "You were the one who shouted at me to wait up. That's why I remembered what Joyce said about shouts. What did you want, Jonas?"

"Not talk, really. I didn't like to see your head bent down, that's all. It's summer in the fields and the sun is only sulking. The mountain laural is blooming and the street is full of beauty."

"Jonas . . . ."

"I know. You don't see what I mean. Well, sure it's a dusty street, but there's six kids playing. Do you know that before this new crop there were ten years when Cedar River was empty of children?"

"What has that to do with me?"

"You're thirty years old, Maurinne, and none of the kids is yours. Why don't you tell the man?"

"What man?"

"You know the man," said Jonas. "You've been turning away from what men there were. I don't blame you. But then the real man comes to town and you know it and yet he's been here for two years and you haven't made a move."

"Jonas," she said, "you don't know what you're talking about and you're interfering and I'm not listening to you . . . ."

"Well, I don't see any hitching line. Don't stay to be polite."

But the world lost some of its brightness to Jonas, too, when Maurinne walked away. Jonas took other people's lethargy in romance as a personal affront.

In Turner's store, he accosted Brent Croswell.

"Is there something wrong with your eyes or with your judgment?" he demanded. "Why don't you stop brooding around and go up to that woman and tell her you love her?"

Brent gasped. He turned red. "How did you . . . .? Jonas, what I do ain't really none of your business."

"Of course it's my business. This whole town is my business. I want happy people in it. I want kids in it. I want love in it."

"Why pick on me?"

"Because you're the one that keeps backing away from the edge," said Jonas. "You're the one that knows what he wants but won't reach for it."

"Jonas," said Clint Reynolds, "you can't run around pairing people up just because you want to see more kids. Brent is fine the way he is. Brent doesn't need a bunch of kids."

"That's right," said Francis Gage. "I think you're talking about that Maurinne Hodges, anyway, and she's some kind of a nut, ain't she? She sure ain't nothing much to look at, neither, and she's snooted every guy that tried to talk to her."

"How would you know somebody was a nut?" asked Brent Croswell. "You ain't got brains enough to barter for a piece of penny candy if they was turned into pure gold."

"I got wallop enough to put your teeth through your tonsils," said Francis. "Go soak your stupid head."

The battle lasted for fifteen exciting minutes. It moved from the area of the pickle barrel to the porch and then to the street. Reggie Gage tried to help his brother and, in fairness, Andy Caruthers had to take on Reggie.

Andy and Reggie fought to a draw but when the main bout ended Francis Gage lay quietly beside the steps. Brent Croswell was erect but bleeding fiercely from the gaps where two teeth had been.

"I don't want to hear anybody else making cracks about Maurinne Hodges," said Brent and he started away. "If they do, they'll have to deal with me."

Jonas Hall smiled in contentment. "That's what I like to see in my town," he said. "I like to see the gentle beginning of an acceptance of love."

Mrs. Kelly says there's always room at the top.
She could be right.
Most folks, knowing their limits,
Would rather see room under them at the bottom.
Who wants to know he's low man,
Serving only to be pointed at?
Who wants to be constantly climbed over
With no one beneath him to climb on?

—*Jonas P. Hall*

Chapter XVII

My father had a favorite comment on inadequacy. It was, "That's the way a sixty-five cent an hour man would do it. Come on, take hold like a dollar and a quarter man."

A dollar and a quarter man in those days was a top mechanic in almost any trade. Wages were scaled down from there. My father was an expert in finding the exact monetary rate for every degree of skill or stupidity.

He set a low price on the efforts of a man who took hold of a hammer halfway up the handle. That practice bothered him more than laziness. He knew that the blow with the choked grip had only half the force and therefore was worth only half as much.

"A workman uses the leverage," he'd say. "Only dubs give up the advantage that's built into the tool."

"But, George," said Uncle Waldron one day, "if I move up a little on the handle I'm more sure of hitting the nail."

"If you start a fight by reaching in and pushing a man's face," said my father, "you'd have a good chance of touching him, too. But you might better put your body behind a full swing and gamble on making contact. Incidentally, there's no such thing as being more sure. Either you're sure or you're not sure. Sure is a positive."

"Moley, moo," said Waldron. "Go watch somebody else. But make up your mind whether you want to correct his carpentry or his grammar, will you?"

"No offense. I just like to keep things straight."

"You sure as hell twist a man up while you're straightening him out," said Waldron. "You'd ought to have been a chiropractor."

The most interesting of my father's wage scale differentiations were on mental capabilities. Mine usually had a low rating.

"That's a sixty-five cent an hour idea," he'd say.

He said it to me quite often. He might have set an even lower rate on some of the things I came up with but he always favored a minimum rate. Sixty-five cents was the lowest humane figure. A man couldn't live on much less and my father didn't want to be in the position of stating that a man wasn't fit to live.

On the other hand, I never heard him exceed his maximum value estimate except when President Wilson was fighting for the League of Nations. "That Wilson," said my father, "has two dollar an hour ideas."

President Wilson might not have been flattered if he had heard this comment. The nation was paying him more than two dollars an hour. But my father meant it as praise, very high praise.

The nearest he came to classifying someone's thinking in a substandard wage bracket was when he spoke of Jesse Hill's wife. Jesse, himself, had no enviable amount of brain power and people in town said he had made a careful effort to find someone even more stupid than he when he decided to get married.

Mrs. Hill had some kind of chronic stomach trouble, the

principal symptom of which was the onset of crippling cramps. She would go into horrible spasms of pain. Her whole body would shake with the muscle tremors.

The baffling thing to Doc Yates was that Mrs. Hill had been downcountry three times to be checked out and even the specialists could find nothing wrong. Her problem was probably psychosomatic. No one could cope with that in those days. What Doc Yates did was give her an opiate. Once quieted, she'd be all right for a month or so.

But before Mrs. Hill would send for Doc Yates, she would suffer her pain for the hour or so it took her to sweep and mop and dust and scrub, following the local rule, "Never let the doctor come into a dirty house."

This cleaning festival was bad enough but Mrs. Hill had another pre-doctor duty that was even more demanding of physical effort. She had to tuck her love letters away.

The love letters were to John Gilbert. Mrs. Hill had never mailed them. She had written them and saved them. She thought this was a secret but Cedar River was too small for secrets.

Mrs. Hill had always wanted to speak loving words to her husband, but Jesse figured that once a man said, "I love you," to his wife he'd said it and he didn't need to say it again. His wife should have heard it the first time.

After all, a man wasn't a damn parrot.

But Mrs. Hill liked romantic phrases. She couldn't get Jesse to listen to them so she wrote them to John Gilbert.

That was the stack of love letters that she disposed of every time her cramps doubled her up and made each movement a battle against fainting.

The big problem with the letters was that she wanted them destroyed in case she died. But if she didn't die, she wanted to be able to get them out occasionally and read them. So she hid them in a place where she was sure they'd never be found unless she went after them herself.

What she did was drag the long ladder out from under the barn, prop it against the big oak tree in the front yard, and climb up about 20 feet to where she could tuck the letters in a crevice.

When they were placed there, she knew that the first storm would turn them into a sodden unreadable mess if she didn't get well and put them back in her bureau drawer.

My father, like many other people, knew the details of this whole deal. He was imaginative enough to know what agonies Mrs. Hill must suffer in her ladder placing, tree climbing, ladder returning routine.

I think he underwent sympathetic spasms, because he always swore when he condemned her self torture.

"That woman," he'd say. "That insane woman and her quiet stupid husband . . . damn, damn, damn . . . their thinking is worse than an acclimated ape's. It isn't worth . . . ."

Then he would stop. The sixty-five cent minimum was inviolate. He couldn't classify Mrs. Hill and Jesse.

The difference in men
Is not that some fail because of errors they make.
It's that some succeed by taking advantage
Of the errors others make.

That's what I told the youngsters
The time I taught Sunday School.
I said, "Don't worry if you strike out
When you're trying to hit a home run for Jesus.
But pure damnation waits for you
If you don't run like Hell for base
When you lift an easy fly.
The Devil might drop the ball."

They said they needed teachers,
But they fired me.
Too bad.
I had a lot more lessons to give,
All useful against the Devil
Or any stray adult,
Or one disguised as the other.

—Jonas P. Hall

Chapter XVIII

Clint Reynolds, the Postmaster, was one of the few solid citizens of Cedar River. Clint found his happiness in the realms of rigidity. His authorities were truisms and platitudes. His final defense against argument was the Bible.

Clint didn't want the Bible to be treated as a guide to philosophy. He considered it to be an encyclopedia of fact, a fortress of absolute truth.

He could take the manual of instruction for Postmasters and interpret certain rules in a manner that was more suitable for Cedar River. He could justify this with his conscience by explaining that there was no such thing as universal wisdom.

In the case of the Bible, however, Clint was not flexible. He needed the Good Book for a barrier against all uncertainties in history, morality, and politics. Its guidance was the anchor of his happiness and his happiness was one of the constancies of Cedar River.

In a region of unpredictable men, Clint Reynolds was outstandingly placid, dependably considerate, and kind. The traces of a smile stayed always on his mouth.

That was why Mrs. Reynolds was jolted one night when Clint came home to supper with a scowl on his face and thunder in his bearing. He ate quietly. He had only two pieces of pie.

His wife was still wondering what could have happened when Clint ended her chance to question. He didn't ease back from the table and light a cigar. He rose and put on his hat.

"Going upstreet," he said. "Might be right back. Might be late. Might have some big things to do."

He headed at a half-trot for the home of the Reverend Adams. "If you could come out on the porch," he said to the minister, "I'd like to tell you something."

It wasn't an invitation. It was a command. It was voiced in a way that let the Reverend Adams know that if there were any difficulty in his getting out on the porch, Clint was prepared to carry him. So the Reverend scraped his pudding dish and obliged.

Clint didn't stop for socializing. He came to the point. "There's too thin a barrier between us and Hell over by Trembley's south hill," he said.

"Trembley's hill?"

"Yeah. They cut into the bottom of it for the gravel for the new road. They've taken out a couple of hundred loads. I want you to get them to put it back."

"It's Trembley's gravel," said the minister.

"I know that. But it's our cover over Hell. And it's thin. The Devil is pushing some of his creatures up through the crust. So far, I think they've all died... probably too cold for them... but now that the top of the hill is gone, they'll start popping right out. They'll take over the town."

The Reverend Adams looked at Clint Reynolds. Clint held out his hand. There was a perfect trilobite in it, unbroken and clear, separated from the rock which had formed around it when the sea had deposited its sediment, millions of years before.

TREMBLEY'S
HiLL

"I got it out of the bottom of that pit," said Clint. "Reverend, it couldn't have crawled down from the top. That hill's a good hundred feet high. The Devil pushed it through from underneath. The crust is thin. Are you going to allow things like this to be pushed out of hell to spread sin?"

The Reverend Adams sighed. "Clint," he said, "I don't believe that's the Devil's messenger."

"What is it then?"

"It's an old life form. It's a bug of some kind and it was probably there before the hill was built up."

"The Lord made the hill," said Clint. "Bible said so. Lord made the mountains and the fields. Why would *he* put a bug under a hundred feet of gravel?"

"Oh, dear," said the minister. "Oh, my, my. Clint . . . Clint . . . *look* . . . I know the answer. That tortured thing tried to escape. It wasn't pushed. The Devil saw it climbing into a crevice and he smote it, but it still had hope enough to climb through miles of crust before it died."

"It was *escaping*?"

"Yes, Clint, but its fate proves that there's no escape from Hell."

Clint thought that over. Then he nodded. "Thanks," he said. He went home and ate another piece of pie. He smiled his old smile. His world was neatly arranged again.

I never meant to eavesdrop
On Bobby Trembley.
He came into the barn
Where I was sleeping on a pile of hay.
When he shouted, I woke up.
Then I heard who he was speaking to
And I hated to have him know I was there.
That was how it was.

He said, "Listen, Satan,
Listen to me.
You shouldn't punish me in Hell, Satan.
You should take it easy on me,
Because I'm not putting you to the trouble
Of tempting me.
You know that?"

He said,
"You can tempt other boys
With the time you save, Satan.
I don't need tempting.
I got more temptations now
Than I got time to give in to."

—*Jonas P. Hall*

Chapter XIX

We were in our last year of high school when we realized that maturity was closing in. In September, we'd been young enough to think a year would last forever. By Thanksgiving, a small fear was starting in us all, because, even though we didn't want to believe it, we remembered that once the holidays were over, it wasn't really long until Easter, and, after Easter, school was nothing but a whisper and a flash.

"But at least we'll have one more Thanksgiving, one more winter, one more spring," said Peter Collins. "We ought to make this year as special as we can."

"I can't make Thanksgiving very special," I said. "I'll have to sit across from Liz and watch her snare the white meat. I'll have to listen to Aunt Margie tell how thankful we should be for all that lovely turnip and those luscious onions."

"We don't have much luck in raising onions," said Peter.

"Nobody around here has much luck with onions . . . except Uncle Waldron. He can't raise an ear of corn, hardly. He can't get his seed back from his potato patch. But he drops six onion seeds and he gets about fifty bushels of onions. I hate onions."

"I know something special we can do. My old man works on Thanksgiving, just like any other day. We have our big dinner at night. You invite me to your house at noon and I'll invite you to our house at night. We'll have two dinners."

We arranged that with our parents. Nobody cared. What was one more place at a Thanksgiving table?

On Thanksgiving morning, Peter showed up with his gun. "We'll go down to the flow and see if there's a deer around," he said. "That'll be special, if we find a deer."

"Good," I said. "Come in a second while I get my rifle."

On the way out of the kitchen, Peter, holding the door with his free right hand pushed, against the storm door with his left. Before he pushed, we had a small pane of glass in our storm door. After he pushed, we had splinters. My father swore.

"Now, George," said my mother, "it's Thanksgiving day . . . glass can be fixed. Just sweep it up, boys. Don't worry about it."

"I'll get a shovel or something," said Peter. He stepped backwards and kicked over the whole bucket of pig mash. "Golly," he said. "What can I clean that up with?"

"Let it go," said my father. "Let it go, for goodness sakes."

"I want to help," said Peter. "Oh, here's something right on the floor."

He had the piece of cloth in the middle of the mess, wiping vigorously before my mother could stop him.

"Please," she said. "That's my new linen dishtowel. You knocked it off the rack with your gun."

Peter stopped wiping. "Golly," he said.

"Come on," I said to him. "Let's get outdoors before you find a way to ruin the turkey."

As we cleared the porch steps, I could hear my father.

"Thanksgiving or no Thanksgiving," he said, "that kid ought to be confined. He's a menace."

"All boys are capable of clumsiness," said my mother.

"Most of them, though," said my father, "don't work so hard to prove it."

We didn't find a deer. But we were almost back to the road when Peter pointed. "Partridge on that thorn plum," he said. "Bet you can't hit it in the head."

I fired. The partridge dropped.

"Good," said Peter. "We'll take this to your father. That'll give him something to be thankful for."

But we met Jubal Dean, the warden, as we emerged from the woods.

"Hey," said Jubal. "The bird season's over. You boys know that."

We *had* known it, too. We honestly had forgotten.

"I'll have to walk over and see your father," said Jubal to me. "This is going to cost somebody a little money."

My father listened to Jubal. "Who shot the thing?" he asked.

"I did," I said.

"I kinda told him to," said Peter.

"That figures," said my father. "All right, Jubal. We'll see you Monday night at the Justice."

My father didn't look happy when we started eating. "That bird will cost five dollars," he said, "and the window . . ."

"Stop it," said my mother. "Think of Thanksgiving. Think of something to be thankful for."

"I just did," said my father. "I'm thankful that I've got ten thousand feet of green pine boards that need to be stickered and piled. I'm thankful these boys have vacation tomorrow."

"There," I said to Peter. "You wanted to do something special. The frost's in the boards. They'll have to be pried apart. Not many people get to pry lumber apart and pile it on their Thanksgiving vacation. Tomorrow'll be special enough for anybody. Do me a favor. Stay away from me on Christmas."

The Cranston hardware store
Was burglarized.
Somebody stole an automatic
And six bullets.

They had an ex-convict down there.
He was living quietly on Water Street,
Working in the paper mill,
Courting a manicurist.

For those auspicious activities,
They put a watch on him.
They followed him everywhere.

So, they knew right where he was
When the Sunday School Superintendent
Held up the bank,
Shot the guard,
And took off with eighteen thousand dollars.

—*Jonas P. Hall*

Chapter XX

We stood in the Cedar River schoolyard and debated our plans for Halloween. The plans were not ambitious. We were about ten years old and parental supervision was still rigid.

"My old man said if I played any tricks around town I'd have something to remember besides the tricks," said Bobby Seekings.

"I wish we lived in Cranston," I said. "We're too easy to recognize here."

"Let's have a bonfire, anyway," said my cousin Paul. "We could roast some apples. Only thing is, we'd have to hide it."

"How can you hide a bonfire?" asked Florence Coosterman.

I had been about to ask that question, but I wasn't going to let an intruder ask it, especially that particular intruder.

"Go away," I said. "We don't want any dumb girls with us. Go find a broomstick to ride."

"Yeah," said Bobby. "Go get a house to haunt."

"I'm not interested in being anywhere near you," said Florence. "But if I were a brave boy, I know where I'd go to have a bonfire so nobody could see it. I'd go to Miller's Cave."

"You crazy or something?" I asked. "Go to Miller's Cave on Halloween?"

"You're afraid, aren't you?" she asked. "You're afraid of the ghosts from those skeletons. You're a bunch of sissies. I *dare* you to go."

"I'm not afraid of ghosts," said Bobby, lying nobly.

"I'm not either," said Paul, also lying.

"Well, I'm not going to take a dare, especially from a girl," I said, evading the issue.

"Hey, look at old Francis Gage," said Bobby. "He's weaving around already. I'll bet he's going to have enough of a glow by tonight so you won't be able to tell him from a goblin."

"Don't try to change the subject," said Florence. "Are you going to Miller's Cave or not?"

"I don't see as it's any of your business," said Paul, "but I ain't afraid of ghosts, so I guess I'd go except that when I get home I'll probably find out that my sister's sick and I have to keep the fire going or something."

"Boy, what a whopper," said Florence. "I guess I'll go down to the store and tell all the men what a brave bunch of boys are growing up in this town."

That was the final stimulus. We made our pact, while Florence grinned. We agreed to meet at seven o'clock, to stay in the cave for two hours, and to find out what the truth was about the ghost from those skeletons.

That time interval would get us home after our parental deadline, but we told ourselves that probably our parents wouldn't notice the violation, just that once.

They had always noticed and we knew they would notice always, but wishful thinking is not confined to politics.

There was no moon that Halloween. The clouds were blanketed over the stars. The path to Miller's Cave was like a mine shaft with our light probing only a few feet into the blackness and its movement making the shadows stir in the spruces that walled us in.

Somehow I was forced into the lead and at the cave entrance I dictated some terms about that honor.

"If I'm going first," I said, "you stay right close behind me. Maybe Florence has rigged some trick. She was awful anxious to get us to come up here."

"Yeah," said Paul.

"She might even be in there," I said, "waiting to moan at us and make us run. She'd love that. I'll bet she's in there. I'll bet anything. We should have brought a firecracker or something to throw in first."

"We didn't though," said Bobby. "So what'll we do?"

"We could wait out here," said Paul, "until she got hungry and came out."

"She's probably got fifteen or twenty sandwiches in there," I told him. "She wouldn't get hungry before nine o'clock and that's as late as I can stay."

"We'll rush her," said Bobby. "We'll pretend we think she's a witch in Florence's form and that we'll have to burn her up. We'll scare her pants off. She knows witches get burned to death."

"All right," I said, "Let's do that."

They closed up behind me. I started into the cave. It wasn't a big cave, just a few turns and a hollowed-out chamber where the skeletons had been found, years ago. We went quietly. Just before the last turn, I heard something.

I nudged Bobby and we stopped. A soft sighing was coming from the chamber ahead. Someone was going, "Pshooh, Psooah."

"That's Florence," I whispered. "Listen, Paul should block the passage here, in case she dodges us. We'll jump in there together, Bobby."

We eased forward. I pushed the light around the corner and it shone directly on a small figure swathed in some kind of gauze.

Bobby and I jumped at it, yelling in triumph.

The figure seemed almost fluid as it backed away, more in a flow than in a movement. I made a try at a tackle, but I missed. Bobby must have missed, too, because he landed on top of me. We lost the light in the collision and we were just climbing back to our feet when Paul yelled.

"I got her," he shouted. "I got her . . . *Aaahhh* . . . *Ooohh* . . ."

The last two sounds were more screams than shouts. We found the light again and turned it on Paul. He was alone and his face showed pain.

"She did something to my arm," he said. "it's numb."

"You let her get away," said Bobby. "You clumsy dope."

"You feel my arm," said Paul. "It's all cold, even. She pinched it somewhere and it hurts like blazes."

We felt the arm. He was right. It was cold like winter frosted steel. It was as rigid as an icicle.

"We better get to Doc Yates," I said. "If that's a blocked artery or something, you could get blood poisoning and die."

We ran, ignoring the darkness, the spruce shadows, and the tricky path. At the road, Paul stopped us.

"It's tingling now," he said. "The blood must be flowing again. It's all right. It's warm."

"Well, I guess it's too late to go back up there now," I said.

"Yeah," said Bobby.

"I wouldn't go back if it was late or not," said Paul.

The next day, angry but interested in her escape technique, we accosted Florence. She looked genuinely surprised as she denied her presence in the cave. She offered proof, too.

"All last evening," she said, "I was at Alice Monroe's. We had a party with cider and doughnuts and cookies and cocoa. If you don't believe me, you ask her."

I started toward where Alice stood with two other girls over by the fence. Bobby grabbed my shirt.

"What's the matter?" I asked.

"Don't ask Alice if Florence was at her house," he said. "I'm almost sure that Florence is telling the truth, but I'll sleep better if I'm not absolutely positive."

"Sleep better? What are you talking about?"

"Well," he said, "When I tackled that thing last night . . . well . . . Bill, *I didn't miss*. I went right through it. There wasn't anything there . . . not anything at all."

"You think it was a *ghost*?" I asked.

"No," he said. "I think it was Florence. I keep telling myself it was Florence. That's why I don't want to prove it wasn't. I don't want to prove that at all."

"In a practical joke,
The idea is to turn the laugh
Against the guy that thought it up,"
Said Waldron Dodds.
"If you get hit with a fish,
Take it home and eat it."

"Suppose it's a spoiled fish?"
Asked Clint Reynolds.

"You eat it anyway,"
Said Waldron.
"That's a more carefully planned joke,
And you've got to make an extra effort
To keep the joker
From getting the best of you."

—Jonas P. Hall

Chapter XXI

Aunt Margie didn't like peddlers. She said they were crooks. She threw flowerpots at them and slammed doors on their fingers.

She pushed the carpet sweeper man over the porch railing and then pummeled his stomach with his own gadget. Her arms whipped up and down as though she were tamping sod as she scolded the man. She worked her way along him, overlapping each impression with the next.

"You've got a nerve," she said, "to pester helpless women and try to cheat them out of their savings."

She snatched a bucket from the tinware peddler, inverted it over his head and pounded on it with her fists as he ran. He couldn't see anything, so he kept tripping over yard debris and falling down and Aunt Margie kicked the pail to make him get up again so she could chase and pound some more.

"Take your cheap merchandise someplace else to sell," she shouted. "I don't want something that will fall apart the first time it's used."

Aunt Margie said that all peddlers were dishonest because if they were honest they wouldn't have to be peddlers; they could stay in one place and open up a store.

"They only come back once a year," she said, "because it takes their customers that long to forget they were swindled."

There may have been some logic in that argument. There was only pure prejudice in Aunt Margie's concluding assertion.

"Most peddlers have scars," she said. "Men with scars are scoundrels. Look at Al Capone and Fu Manchu. Anytime you see a man with a scar, you can make up your mind he has villainy in his heart. Scars are the mark of Satan."

Since many men in Cedar River had scars and some small few of them were honest, this bias of Aunt Margie's might have been expected to bring debate, but it didn't. Aunt Margie disliked debate.

If anyone had said, "Doc Yates has a scar, and he isn't a villain," Aunt Margie would have said, "I wasn't talking about Doc, of course."

Then she would have spoken scathingly about people who didn't have brains enough to distinguish between men with scars and men with scars, all men being unequal from birth and certain men being entitled by virtue of their blessed inequality to be scarred or non-scarred as they chose, without any adverse effect on their personality or character or esteem earned.

"Moses had a scar, too, but he didn't go from house to house selling tulip bulbs," she would have said.

Even Jonas Hall couldn't have come up with an answer to that.

There was one exception to Aunt Margie's rules about peddlers. She liked the man who sold Furbush brushes. She said he wasn't a peddler at all; he was a gentleman who peddled things.

Back in 1935, the Furbush man had complimented Aunt Margie on the pattern of her apron when she first opened the door. She had listed him, then, as a discerning and artistic man who merited patronage and gentle treatment.

She invited him in for coffee and cookies. She let him sell her brushes for teeth, floors, hair, and bathtub.

"He's genteel," she said. "The Scrubrub Brush man is a rascal. I don't trust the Scrubrub man. I didn't see it happen, but I know he's the one who let his horse eat my petunias."

Aunt Margie was prepared to demonstrate her dislike to the Scrubrub man. She was disappointed at his delay in calling. She had two cracked saucers ready for her first broadside and a broken stovelid to throw as he retreated.

"Just let him come to my door," she said, "and he'll find out exactly what I think of him."

But the Scrubrub man already knew what Aunt Margie thought of him. Mrs. Wheeler had told him. He detoured around Aunt Margie's house, even though he lost custom from Mrs. Benson next door. He didn't want to give up business, but he didn't want to be beaten to death, either.

One day, though, Mrs. Benson left word at Mrs. Wheeler's for the Scrubrub man to call. She said if he kept neglecting her, she was going to write to the company and complain. He had to obey her summons.

Aunt Margie was upstairs, but she happened to look out the window. She saw the Scrubrub wagon and the Scrubrub horse. She moved to her side door and waited, a saucer in each hand. But the Scrubrub man was already safely inside Mrs. Benson's kitchen. It was the Furbush man who approached from the other direction and made a blind landing on the side porch, guided by the beam of confidence engendered by past successes.

Aunt Margie heard his steps. She heard him say, "*Brushes.*"

She opened the door and smacked him full in the face with the saucer. Blood spurted and masked his features. Aunt Margie brought the other saucer down on his head. He started to run. She gave him a few steps distance as a gift before she shouted, "Petunias aren't horse feed," and let him have the stovelid, expertly, sliding it off her hand so that it struck him flat on the back of his head.

Down in the driveway gravel went the Furbush man, his arms outstretched, his body limp.

"I don't want any brushes today," said Aunt Margie.

She slammed the door and went to the icebox to find something for a little snack. Action always made her hungry.

The street loungers carried the Furbush man to Doc Yates. Doc patched and stitched. "That gash on his face is pretty deep," said Doc. "Margie really ought to cut her finger nails before she extends her hospitality."

Observant neighbors guessed what must have happened to bring about this mistake in brush peddler identity. They explained the error to Aunt Margie. She seemed penitent but not inclined to condemn herself completely.

"Little mistakes like that will happen," she said. "Just the other day Waldron put on his Saturday night store shirt to go to church. To err is human. Somebody said that and it's true."

On his next trip, the Furbush man came to Aunt Margie's door expecting apologies and a welcome. He didn't get either. She took one look at him, screamed, and chased him down the walk with a broom.

Mrs. Benson heard the scream and saw the activity. Aunt Margie turned to her and sighed.

"His true nature finally came out," said Aunt Margie. "Did you see his face? He's got a great big *scar*."

Maybe there are places
Where the world laughs with you when you laugh.
That isn't true in Cedar River.
Here they laugh when you have finished laughing.
They laugh at you for having laughed
At times not listed in their books of rules
For being funny.

Laughter not approved by old traditions
Is acceptably hilarious.

—Jonas P. Hall

Interim

We somehow think of the fall in terms of nostalgia, with sober references to the melancholy induced when the daybreak mists burn off to reveal the red and gold of the ridges.

We associate the time of growth's end and dormancy's beginning with the inevitable progression of our own lives from phase to phase.

For the love of seasonal change is a part of living and yet the limitations of life are involved with the number of seasons that do change.

So I suppose what we do, when the frost-touched field grasses whisper themselves from green to brown, is to sum up the beauty of the past, to enlarge on it, to make it more beautiful than it was, even to wish it would repeat itself. Repetition seems desirable not because the past is better than any probable future but only because it has proved to be comparatively harmless to humanity as it took its place in the pageant of time.

A large part of the enjoyment of glory is the distortion of it. In anticipation, there is a glow but there is not yet a fire nor the memory of fire.

Tomorrow may not come.

Yesterday has already been here.

The sorrows of the past cannot be more bitter than they have already been, but who can put a limit on the sorrows of tomorrow?

Fall melancholy may be defensive. It may not be regret for what has been lost. It may be reluctance to add more to the losses that will be mourned in the future.

Autumn air seems clearer and the winds are more personal and the past stands closer to the edge of a curtain that we might reach out and tear apart. But we are afraid to reach. We don't want to ease back into scenes which we may remember as being more attractive than they were.

There never was perfection in Cedar River. That is what a man must remember in the gentle months of autumn, summer, and spring. He must remember it even in the harshness of winter, when he so desperately wants to turn what was into what might have been.

"The world won't ever be as perfect as it should be," said my father. "So I guess it gives a man courage, once in awhile, to think it's the kind of place it isn't."

He was talking to the Reverend Adams. He was making a half hearted defense of Uncle Oscar's statement that the beverages he brewed made the world look better to a hard working man. In that defense he was plagiarizing old Doc Yates.

"Not that Oscar knows anything about the feelings of a hard working man," my father continued. "He's never been one himself. But there may be a place for the inducement of dreams."

In this respect, the minister was more of a realist than my father.

"George," he said, "souls aren't saved by relaxing effort and imagining that results have been obtained. Even if we know we'll never have universal virtue, we have to keep hoping that we will."

The two men had a friendly argument about that for years, agreeing to disagree but having a verbal battle occasionally. They respected each other's convictions.

But neither of them respected Jonas Hall's opinions on the subject. Jonas wasn't in favor of either dreaming of perfection or striving for it. He didn't even approve of perfection.

"Nothing could be duller than universal perfection," he said, "except maybe universal virtue."

In a time and a town of lip service to high moral concepts, even on the part of those who were furthest from the practice of the virtues publicly admired, Jonas had few supporters.

He didn't care.

"Think of what you'd lose in a perfect world," he said. "There wouldn't be any humor, for one thing. We do all our laughing either at error or in error, don't we? And most of our talking is about error, anticipated with joy or condemned with sorrow."

When these statements were attacked, Jonas could make the attackers angry enough to walk away by saying, "Can you think of a less interesting group of people than a gang that had nothing to say to each other on Saturday at the store except that they and their friends were perfect . . . praise the Lord, Amen."

Folks didn't even want to stay around when he talked like that. They were afraid they might agree with Jonas and they were afraid of the effect of agreement on their souls.

Jonas had one advantage over his opponents. They feared that they would never see world perfection come into target range. Jonas didn't have to fear that he would.

I suspect that our town resented Jonas' happiness about the probable continued absence of perfection more than they resented Uncle Oscar's refusal to work toward it and his preference for deluding himself into dreams of its presence.

With Oscar, folks knew where they stood. He didn't confuse them. They could look down on his weaknesses.

With Jonas, they didn't know whether to look down or up. Their belief in their own superiority became precarious.

The natural result of this was that Jonas was a more desirable verbal target for the yearners toward virtue than was Oscar. But the worst thing about this contest for desirability or undesirability was that the two men often spent an evening together. No one knew what they could find to talk about but everyone thought that there should be laws against it.

Mrs. Wheeler went so far as to upbraid Jonas for this association.

"He'll convert you completely to sin," she said, managing to give the impression that Jonas, although strange, might still be snatched from the brinks.

"I never found out for sure," said Jonas, "what sin is. Seems as though it varies according to the social rating of who's involved."

Mrs. Wheeler had an answer to that. "You come to church Sunday," she said, "and the Reverend Adams will tell you what's a sin and what's not. He knows."

Jonas smiled, shook his head, and walked away. I saw that he was headed for Oscar's house and I followed along. I was about 12 years old at that time and my parents were not enthusiastic about my association with Oscar, so naturally I visited him whenever I could.

Oscar was stirring honey and yeast and elderberries into a sweet cider base, preparing some new beverage that he probably hoped would be a glory previously unattained.

"Mrs. Wheeler says you're a sinner," said Jonas.

"That ain't no news flash," said Oscar.

"I suppose she thinks I'm one, too."

"You probably are. Why don't you wash out them jars while you're waiting?"

"Mrs Wheeler," said Jonas, "sees sin as a coat you can put on or take off. She sees salvation as a long line of people waiting to repent. She sees joy in the hearts of the saved."

"You take a million gallons of something like I'm putting together right now," said Oscar, "and you'd bring joy to the world like Mrs. Wheeler never dreamed."

"Take more than a million gallons. It would take a million times a million, even if you rationed sinners to one sip."

"No reason you couldn't have that many. Put the righteous

in the fields to pick the fruit and the berries. Think of all them things, ripe and waiting for proper treatment to make folks happy."

That was Oscar's fall vision, the bounty of nature ripening and filling long lines of baskets carried to presses or carts winding along pleasant lanes toward brandy vats.

"The trouble with your remedy," said Jonas, "is that it's temporary. Come on, Bill I'll walk you home before you get converted to pagan notions that Mrs. Kelly will have to wallop out of you."

As we wandered away, he was meditating aloud.

"Your uncle isn't wrong in one way," he said. "The righteous are apt to be grim. But there are lots of grim sinners, too, and I doubt that you'd lead them toward virtue by filling them with elderberry wine."

Blessings come from God.
Mrs. Wheeler knows that.
She accepts it.
She only feels that God should recognize
Her place as middleman.

Why should God drop manna on the Gages
When she will put a basket for them in the store
And even prime sweet charity's slow pump
With an orange and a can of beans?

—Jonas P. Hall

Chapter XXII

Randy Gage was a big hairy bear of a man. He married a sweet and gentle schoolteacher, a classic blue-eyed blond who weighed about 100 pounds and had the kind of charm that might have made a swarm of bees bring their honey to her instead of to the hive.

Cedar River jokesmiths called the pair "Beauty and the Beast," not highly original but definitely applicable. But Randy didn't care what he was called and neither did Lily. They moved into what an uncritical person would call a house and they started to have children. They had so many, they lost count. Randy's one ambition was to be an ancestor. He achieved it.

Lily's goal was to keep her children around her. She was fairly successful. All the Gages got along beautifully together, so the girls brought their husbands home to live and the boys did the same with their wives.

Prudence Gage did move out when she married Tom Webster. Pearl left when she married Joe Caruthers. The rest stayed. They liked informality. They enjoyed knowing that responsibility for food and fuel was so widely shared.

The Gages did have outside jobs sporadically. They all fished and hunted. Fathers, mothers, and children worked in the big Gage gardens and whole platoons of Gages went out ferning every year. Francis gathered balsam sap. Reggie had a little shingle mill. Faith's husband tended 50 laying hens.

Basically, though, the family belonged to the cult of immediacy. If there were food for dinner today, who cared about tomorrow? But after one series of more than usually precarious winters, Lily Gage reluctantly became a commissary sergeant. She didn't want to have to keep saying, "Nothing," when someone asked her what there was to eat that night.

Late spring and summer and early fall posed no problems for the Gages. Someone was always picking something or bringing home salvage from a resort hotel kitchen or even dropping a few bills in the store food kitty. In late September, though, Lily began to demand that every resident couple or single adult put something in the storehouse for winter use each day.

She kept up this demand all through October and those were the days when all Gages had to be watched more closely than usual. Some of the stored fodder was legitimate, needing only the contribution of effort. Potatoes and apples were harvested. Root cellars were filled with turnips, carrots, and beets. The girls salted down cabbage, waterglassed eggs, and dried beans.

But men who were late in bringing their sheep down from summer pastures might have one young one less than they figured on. And Mr. Turner did have to move his molasses barrel one year from its normal position near the back wall because someone bored a hole right through wall and barrel, lowering the contents by five gallons or so.

"Don't want to make no accusations," said Turner, "but Francis Gage did a lot of pacing in that corner and the hole was bored plumb center."

There were obvious raccoon droppings near the back of Deak Trembley's corn crib but Deak said he didn't know how the coons removed a board so neatly or carried off so much in one night.

After two years of Lily Gage's mandated storage splurges, almost everyone in town knew what Lily had accomplished by way of ensuring winter food. There was some admiration but there was also some resentment. Mrs. Wheeler thought the minister should talk to Lily. The Reverend Adams was reluctant but he finally asked my father what he thought about it.

"I wouldn't bother," said my father. "In general, there's no greater drain than there was in the years before Lily began to make positive preparations for the hungry months."

"People seem to think there's a drain," said the minister.

"There isn't. Before Lily took hold, everyone knew that the Gages were going to be hungry or maybe worse than that in January. People said they deserved it, served them right, let them starve. But still the Christmas food donations kept building up. I've seen years when it took six strong men to carry the boxes."

"But if that took care of needs, why wasn't it better?"

"Depends on which side you're on," said my father. "It was better for the givers. They got the glow of grace. The way it is now is better for the Gages. Makes them feel self-reliant."

"You're condoning dishonesty," said the minister. "You're contradicting your own ethical codes."

"If a man can't live with contradictions," my father told him, "then he shouldn't live in a town like this. You know that."

The Reverend Adams did know it, so he ended the discussion. He had learned to accept guidance in the intricacies of tolerance.

Strangers have trouble with that. Learned observers and philosophers have trouble with it. Admittedly, it is confusing. Tolerance in a small town involves more than lip service. There are so few people that none of them can be crossed off the books of friendship just because they have a bunch of undesirable characteristics.

Nowhere is the old adage about accepting what cannot be changed more applicable than in rurality. That was why my

Uncle Oscar wasn't a complete pariah. Folks didn't forgive his sins but they tolerated them, assuming their continued presence but understanding that they might have been worse. And Oscar did have some value. He could be pointed out to small boys as an example of what they could become if they disobeyed their parents.

Newcomers could be startled by town casualness toward Oscar's actions. They might even go to Jesse Hill, the town policeman, to complain that someone had put the snatch on five pounds of sugar that they had left in a car while they went into the Post Office.

Jesse wasn't about to take action on these minor offenses. He'd say, "Probably Oscar. Listen, even Gabriel has stopped trying to keep a full account book on Oscar. You just gotta remember to watch him, that's all. If you do, you won't have no trouble with him."

The strangers would shake their heads. Then they might try to isolate themselves completely from Oscar. That was another error. Just because they stayed away from him, that didn't mean he'd stay away from them.

Aunt Margie was another example. She'd had bitter battles with everyone in town. In a larger place, she would have had no friends left. In Cedar River, however, even the women that Margie had been forced to smack with a handful of potato salad at a church supper knew she was a valuable member of the missionary fundraising group. So they let her forgive them.

Public opinion favored this treatment and Cedar River people were great for public opinion as long as it didn't interfere with their own enjoyment of specific sins.

That was what threw newcomers off balance, the combination of acceptance and defiance. It was hard to understand that some persons were permitted certain sins, that other persons were permitted other sins, and that the only basis for absolute condemnation was an attempt by persons in one category to infringe on the privileges of those in another.

Thus Clint Reynolds couldn't have made off with someone's shovel without being called a public menace and a crook. But Francis Gage was expected to try to steal shovels or axes or even stove legs and if he got away with it, that was the fault of the owner of the gear.

Because it had long been understood that, "you gotta watch them Gages." An unwatched Gage was a potential threat. But nobody expected to have to watch Clint Reynolds so Clint would have been taking an unfair advantage if he had stolen something.

I suspect that this moral code was more practical than praiseworthy. That didn't matter as long as no one tried to export it and I can't remember that anyone ever did.

I smile when reading that the sages say,
"There is no black nor white but only gray."
That may apply in Persia or Tibet
Remoter places haven't heard it yet.

—Jonas P. Hall

Chapter XXIII

Peter Saunders and his wife, Peggy, were welcomed new residents of Cedar River. People liked them. They fitted.

Cedar River, after all, didn't have much to offer to immigrants. It was granted space for its existence by a sweeping bend in the river and a break in the lower ridge chain. Prosperity always passed it by. Depressions never did.

But Peter and Peggy were attached to the town because it had been the scene of their courtship, itself a wild adventure which involved the whims of the hill gods, the thrust of summer love, a poker game which ended in a fight, and the burning of a garage.

All that is another story, bound in another book beside the skidding of Minnie Trembley from the brook bed and the winter of Uncle Waldron's yellow horse. It needs no telling here.

Married and moved into an attractive house by Cedar River

standards, Peggy Saunders eased into the life of the town as though her place had always been there waiting for her.

She learned whose butter to buy and whose to let Mr. Turner ship downriver out of town. She learned the knack of being direct and devious at the same time. She found out what was unforgivable conduct for a woman. Unorthodoxy was accepted. Moral error was not.

Cedar River women were not supposed to make eyes at other women's husbands or to let their children do things that other women forbade theirs to do.

In the contributions that a woman made to at least four of the six community suppers, there was supposed to be some meat in the casserole or some eggs in the cake.

Possession of more than one "good dress" was not allowed. Neither was too rapid replacement of the good dress unless catastrophe befell its owner. Some women couldn't afford a new good dress every year and the other women were supposed to guide their buying accordingly.

That dress code did not apply to aprons, however. Most women had a half-dozen good aprons. That was because aprons were bought at the Ladies' Aid "sales of work" and buying was not an act of status seeking but one of commendable charity.

No woman was supposed to call on another woman after seven o'clock on Sunday evening. It was understood that decent housewives would be busy after that time, doing the washing that they would hang up early Monday morning and pretend to have done before they cooked breakfast.

Penalties for defiance of this conduct code were severe. When my cousin Susan was married to Andy Parsons, she kissed young Gert Trembley's Joseph too hard at a husking bee one night and she had to wear the same "best dress" for three years to atone for the sin.

"She stayed right tight to him for a good three minutes," said Mrs. Turner. "There's no excuse for that kind of behavior."

Actually, there was an excuse, but Susan never admitted that fact. Susan was stubborn in some ways.

What happened was that when Susan got a red ear and so had to kiss someone, she headed for Joseph out of kind-heartedness. He was the most homely man in town and a bit dim-witted besides. Susan was sure no other red corn discoverer would pick him, so she did.

But when Joseph realized that he had some action coming, he tried to park his gum behind his ear. He had been out too many times to bring in corn and tap the jug in the barn. He missed his ear and put the gum on his cheek. The lights were dim enough so that Susan didn't see the gum and that was where she kissed him. She got stuck and had to bite the gum off and take it with her.

There was no rule against chewing secondhand gum in Cedar River, but there was such a thing as pride. Susan kept quiet and paid the penalty and eventually she was forgiven.

All these things Peggy Saunders had to learn and she did learn them. She was cheerful, energetic, and sincere. The women agreed that her college education hadn't destroyed her common sense and so had not done her any permanent harm.

Peggy got along so very well that the women were really upset when she told them, one year, that she and Peter were closing their house for three months because Peter had agreed to spend January through March cleaning up a poorly run log job in the upper Cold Stream country.

"Peter will have his headquarters in a town called Holy Gate," she said. "Do you know anything about that place?"

"A little smaller than our town," said Mrs. Reynolds. "Settled by some Millerites after the world didn't come to an end. They sold their farms in Tennessee when they were getting ready to go to heaven. Then, when they didn't, they moved up here."

"Andy and I stayed there for two days when he was selling harness," said Susan Parsons. "Keep a sour pickle in your mouth, so you'll look as though you belonged. That place is so sanctimonious that it would probably snub Gabriel because all musicians are immoral."

"It's only for three months," said Peggy. "I'll be all right. I don't have to impress the women."

"I'm afraid you should, dear," said Mrs. Turner. "If you're the weekly hissing at the sewing club, the effect will come back in the amount of work that Peter gets out of the men."

"So," said Peggy, "I'll try to be a short-term saint."

She did well at it, too. The women of Holy Gate watched her, then accepted her. In their untalented way, they even tried to be kind to this stranger from a heathen culture. Two of them, after much effort, managed to smile at Peggy one morning at the store.

Peggy might have moved away leaving a semi-favorable impression on the pious had the company accountant not been taken ill just as the job was closing down. The substitute sent to make a final tally of costs, cords, and unused supplies was a capable secretary-bookkeeper. But she was also a beautiful blond and her kilted skirt was a good two inches above her knees.

The Holy Gate women gasped as Peter escorted the secretary into the company office. At eleven o'clock, the two were still in there alone. At noontime, the same condition existed.

A four-women delegation, tight lipped and cold eyed, marched to the Saunder's apartment over the general store. The women told their story, their excitement rising as they described the probable activity at the office.

"For your own good," they said, "we thought you ought to know."

It was that phrase that snapped the twine on Peggy's package of super-piety. It was then that she decided that these poor souls deserved something really juicy, something that would be a glorious memory, always, as they traded future bland gossip.

"Well, thank you," she said. "But I don't have any actual right to control Peter. We're not married. We just live together."

Then, as they hurried away to compete in the spreading of this prize information, Peggy started to pack.

Mrs. Wheeler runs the missionary fund.
She always has.
Other ladies manage other charities,
Each one assigned.
Confusion comes when volunteers step in.
A volunteer might squeeze a quarter through the lining
Of the hat he passes.
Cedar River knows who can be trusted.
No others need apply.

—Jonas P. Hall

Chapter XXIV

One of the hardest things to do in any small town is to escape a family reputation. That was the problem that Kenneth Gage faced. He was a hard worker and a born giver. By heritage, he had no right to be either one.

Prudence and Pearl Gage had proved that a Gage daughter, if caught early enough by a respectable husband, could be "un-Gaged" and so turned toward responsibility and virtue. But Kenneth started defying Gageness on his own hook when he was just a small boy.

Kenneth carried groceries. He helped people mow lawns. He washed milk cans for Deak Trembley.

These actions didn't indicate a desire to earn money. He was never rewarded with anything more than a cookie or a kind word. So Kenneth confused all the adults in town. They couldn't explain why a Gage would volunteer to work. Most of them figured there was something wrong with his head but a few credited him with having some ulterior motive that would eventually come out.

Actually, what Kenneth Gage had was an immense capacity for taking on himself the problems of other people. No one in Cedar River could believe this was a possible condition.

"A Gage is a Gage," said my Uncle Oscar. "Blood is blood. That's what I always say."

The men in the store assembly nodded, even though most of them believed that Oscar's blood wasn't blood at all but a solution of alcohol and red dye. They knew Oscar wasn't talking about his blood but about blood in general.

In the outside world, people can talk about genes. In the hill country the reference has always been to blood. The blood of every family line had specific character-forming ingredients.

This was a very handy belief to have. It excused weaknesses and it permitted a downgrading of accomplishment. If a man habitually let his fences deteriorate, it would be remembered that his grandfather was no great hand with fences either. Fence neglect was in the man's blood.

Ned Burns had the best corn in town, year after year, but no one had to go to the trouble of studying Ned's methods. Corn growing was in the Burns blood. No man could be upbraided for not being able to compete with what was in another man's blood.

This was such a comforting theory that children picked it up early. One of the young Nelsons tried to extend its acceptance to school, but he learned that there was a difference between folklore and academic credence.

He hadn't done his homework and he said, "I forgot, I'm absentminded. All the Nelsons are absentminded."

"That's interesting," said Mrs. Kelly. "Well, then we'll have to work hard, won't we, to see to it that you're the first Nelson that isn't."

She walloped him about five times and he decided he could prove she was wrong. He decided that he could become a non-absentminded Nelson without any more work at all.

But when almost every adult in a town believes in the power of good blood and bad blood, a few defiers of the belief don't make much impression. So suspicion of Kenneth Gage's motives for helping people never did end.

"He's deep," said the men at the store. "He's got plans."

That attitude should have turned Kenneth into a challenger of his own humanitarian impulses. It didn't. He retained his concern. He kept trying to demonstrate it.

He was about 18 when he offered to help Ted Carter.

Ted was an old bachelor who lived out on the Big Brook road. He didn't have much except a garden patch, a pig, a woodlot, a horse, a cow, and a hayfield. He took sick one winter and he didn't seem to be able to gain strength through the spring and into the summer.

He came into town in mid-July, just when everyone was busy with this and that. He expressed his need for help.

"Can't pay much," he said, "but I can pay a little. Ain't looking for no charity. I got to get my hay cut and I never finished bringing out my wood before I commenced to feel poorly."

The men hesitated. If there had been drama involved, such as a sudden widowhood or a fire, they would have ganged up and helped. But this seemed more like the offer of a job and they didn't need jobs. They were all busy. They were inclined to stall.

Kenneth Gage, however, offered himself. "I'll help you out for a couple of weeks," he said, "and it won't cost you anything. I got a little time to spare. We're pretty well caught up at home."

Ted Carter thanked him, accepted his offer, and went home. That night, the men voiced their suspicions. They decided to act.

"No Gage helps a man for nothing," they said. "It ain't in his blood. Kenny is probably figuring on stealing half that wood and most of the hay. We'd ought to get over there and see that he doesn't. Any man should take time to keep decent citizens from being robbed."

So the next day, there were eight men and four horses in the Carter hayfield watching and helping Kenny. It took only three days to fill the barn. Then the men helped Kenny in the woods so they could be sure he didn't take any of the stump-piled firewood out the back way, to be added to Kenny's own winter supply.

There were so many scoot loaders and unloaders and fitters and pilers that they got in each other's way. They set up what was almost a conveyer belt from the woods to the stacks in the shed. Then, just to make sure that Kenneth wouldn't have any excuse to come back and maybe steal a few tools, they cleaned out the stable and the tie-up in good shape and spread the manure on the fallow land that would be next year's tillage.

When they left, Ted Carter said, "Thank God for my good neighbors."

Back in the store that evening, the men laughed and said, "We sure kept that Gage kid from getting away with anything."

Kenneth Gage ate supper with his sister Prudence and her husband, Tom Webster. Kenny said, "You know, those guys worked so hard that I didn't have a chance to help half as much as I meant to."

"Good solid bunch," agreed Tom. Then he shook his head at Prudence because he knew what he was sure she was going to say should not be said.

The drama of this life
Depends on timing.
That's why we have to be denied previews.
If we were able to anticipate defenses,
Virginity would be a concept
Unknown to civilized society.

I suspect it will be shortly, anyway;
And, having no personal stake in the matter,
I'd vote either way.

—Jonas P. Hall

Chapter XXV

At Cedar River family reunions and other assorted festivals, children were always brought onto center stage by prodding parents and forced to recite, dance, or sing.

The performances were always horrible but the assembled adults usually managed to come up with some sort of expression that made the parents feel that their children might have a future in the entertainment world.

The most ingeniously contrived semi-compliment was one that Clint Reynolds dredged up in desperation when he was sitting next to my uncle Waldron while Waldron's son, Paul, was singing.

Paul had no singing ability at all. He bellowed in a rasping monotone, changing tune and pitch sporadically. Unhappily, the only song he knew was one of those old ballads that had about twenty-five verses. Paul was singing the chorus between each audience numbing verse.

Clint Reynolds kept fidgeting. Uncle Waldron kept looking at him, expecting him to say something, beginning to wonder if Clint were some kind of a barbarian who lacked both politeness and art appreciation.

Clint finally found the words that kept friendship in being. He turned toward Waldron and said, “Holds out good, don’t he?”

Waldron accepted this tribute to durability as a sign of approval.

Clint, of course, didn’t blame Paul for trying to sing when singing was beyond his power. No adult at one of these gatherings ever assumed that the performances were volunteered.

In the case of Mrs. Trembley, however, the situation was different. She was a free adult and she was not drafted. She volunteered. Anytime she was present at a party, she thwarted all attempts to sidetrack her. She was positive that everyone wanted to hear her sing and she didn’t intend to disappoint the crowd.

She sang, she always said, “by request,” but no one ever found out who did the requesting. Had there been such a person and had he been discovered, he undoubtedly would have been found floating in the river some day, disguised as a stick of pulpwood.

Mrs. Trembley even gave her unknown admirer credit for naming her song. She would say, “I am now going to sing ‘Annie Laurie,’ by request.”

It didn’t really matter what she sang. She had no singing voice. The only differences between her songs were the words.

I remember my father’s speaking to my mother in despair after one of Mrs. Trembley’s tortuous performances at the Turner’s Silver Wedding celebration.

“Why does a supposedly merciful Heaven permit that woman to persist in her folly?” he asked.

“That’s not very kind,” said my mother.

“Neither is her determination to start a migraine epidemic.”

“Stop fussing about it,” said my mother. “Let her sing if she wants to sing. She’s a very generous person and she works hard at the church suppers.”

My father was seldom startled by feminine logic, but he was that time. He confided in me later.

"Bill," he said, "I'm beginning to think that most of the rules I've taught you about conduct are only applicable in theory. We seem to be living in an age where generalities are excuses for specifics."

"I don't understand that," I said.

"You will. There's always been so much insanity in the world that some of it had to be overlooked because the asylums were full. But since women got the vote, insanity is being legalized. We're going to have Joan Calligans popping up all over the place."

"You don't like Miss Calligan?"

"I think she's a fine dedicated lady," he said. "I do find it hard, though, to believe that because a boy doesn't live in the best house in town or get a new bicycle for Christmas he's justified in setting fire to a warehouse and shooting a policeman."

"Does Miss Calligan believe that?"

"I don't know," said my father. "I don't dare ask her."

I dropped the subject but I didn't understand that last remark, either. No one ever had to ask Joan Calligan what she believed. She gave her opinions without being asked.

Joan was the target of Mrs. Kelly's scorn when Joan voiced a theory about Uncle Oscar that Mrs. Kelly thought was detrimental to the concept of self-discipline. Joan said Oscar's drinking was a sickness.

"You've got the log pulling the horse," said Mrs. Kelly. "He drinks because he's a bum and he's sick because he drinks."

Joan tried to quote some authorities. Mrs. Kelly wasn't interested. "You bring those smart alecks up here," she said, "and I'll straighten them out on drinking. I know more about drinking than anyone has a right to know. My late husband, God rest him, although I don't believe God is resting him, nor should, either, but then, who am I to know more than God and I'm the first to admit it, was a drinker and fell off the log boom and yet there you are trying to tell me that Oscar isn't a bum. Sick, my foot . . . and I should let you have the full force of it for your atheistic notions."

While Mrs. Kelly was saying all this, she was backing Joan Calligan up toward the corner of the Post Office lobby and Joan was undoubtedly wondering why her doctor had told her that if she moved to a small town for a year she would give her nerves a rest.

That was why Joan was in Cedar River. She was a psychologist from Boston. She had probed too many disordered minds and was beginning to challenge her own ideas about normality. A doctor today would probably have put her on some mild sedative and kept her working but in those early days of psychiatry, mercy tempered tranquillizers.

Unhappily, Joan brought her work dedication with her when she settled into the old Jenkins house. She should have tucked her training away and enjoyed life. She couldn't do it. She began to upset locally accepted ideas, particularly those involving reasons for child misbehavior.

Every adult in town knew why small boys were obnoxious. It was because they were not yet old enough to overcome their barbaric heritage. They had not yet learned that they were supposed to pretend to be civilized.

Even my father believed this. I was about nine or ten at that time, old enough to be the subject of my father's attention when he had to muse aloud without argument, but not old enough to be fully trusted with the musing. Sometimes my father carried his complaints about the town's sanity too far and then he would catch himself and tell me he was not interested in being quoted.

"If I am," he once said, "I won't have to hire Sherlock Holmes to find the source. A word to the wise . . . right?"

I wasn't very wise, but I was wise enough for that word.

All of that has little to do with Joan Calligan. Joan recommended reasoning with unruly children instead of smacking them out of savagery and into civilization. This notion pitted her against all parents and against the Reverend Adams, a kind man but one who believed that impulses inspired by Satan must be driven out of boys with a strap.

Joan won one victory at our house. It was a victory that convinced me that if there were not some truth in her ideas there should be. She saved me from deserved punishment.

Ever since I had been able to tell the taste of one thing from another, I had been a patsy for mustard pickles. I loved them. Noting my affection and following the customs of the time, my mother had decreed that mustard pickles were not good for me.

The accepted ideas about food for small boys, in the 1920s, was that if they liked it it was undoubtedly indigestible, weakening, and an enemy of their stomachs.

If a boy found some type of food repulsive, however, then that food was assumed to be a blood purifier, a body builder, and a bone strengthener. To stay healthy, a boy was supposed to eat things that he could hardly force down his throat.

So my mustard pickle ration was about half a chunk of cauliflower a week. That didn't satisfy the craving. It only kept the craving alive. It reminded me that the wonderful taste of mustard pickles was not imaginary but real.

I'm not sure why Joan Calligan and the Reverend Adams came to dinner at the same time. I suspect that Joan was invited and that the minister dropped in for a call and was therefore included. There was a rumor around town, anyway, that the Reverend Adams had a nose for fried chicken that was the equivalent to that of a bird dog for partridge. We were having fried chicken that night.

Whatever the reason for our having two guests, we all sat down at the table and bowed our heads to hear the minister say grace. I noted that I had been presented with a bonanza. The dish of mustard pickles was nudging my plate.

The minister went to work. So did I. Before he had even warmed to his task, I had snaffled two little onions and a piece of cucumber. Before the "Amens" I had emptied half the pickle dish. No adult disturbed me. For an adult to open his eyes during grace would have been to admit that his whole attention was not on thankfulness for bounty received. Even worse, it would have meant that he didn't trust divinity to keep discipline.

Circumstantial evidence was my undoing. Mustard pickles drip. The trail led across my plate. I had a slight smear on my chin.

My father sighed, stood up, and said, "Come on, Bill."

The minister nodded his agreement with the smiting that seemed to be in store. Joan Calligan protested.

Joan said, "Surely you aren't going to punish him. Children are notified by nature of their bodily deficiencies. His system was probably crying out for some missing chemical component."

"Nonsense," said the minister. "Bodily cravings are sinful and unnatural. You'll notice, young lady, that children never crave things that don't taste good. Their greed prompts their craving."

"How about a craving for plain garden dirt?" asked Joan. "Yesterday, I saw a boy deliberately eating dirt. His system was telling him it needed nitrogen or potassium or some trace element."

"Hmpff," said the minister.

But my father sat down again. "There might really be something in that idea," he said. "An ailing dog does eat grass."

My father was seldom conned, but he was that time. He forgot his own maxim that one instance doesn't make a proof. And I did know quite a lot about Joan Calligan's dirt eating case.

The boy she had seen eating dirt was Bobbie Trembley. He was eating it because, an hour before, on a double double dare, he had eaten a worm while it was still wriggling and he wanted to give it something to burrow in so it wouldn't make a hole in his stomach.

But I didn't tell my father that. Instead, I asked gently, "Could I have some more pickles, please?"

"Don't push your luck," said my father, "even with scientific backing. You might find that, later tonight, your system will crave a shot of castor oil."

A boy can start at six to swindle his schoomates.
He can advance by degrees
From short changing paper route customers
To selling used cars.
Then, just as he has become a respected citizen,
Given the job of passing the collection plate,
He may turn honest, reporting every dime.
Having thus embarrassed previous plate passers
By the dramatic jump in donation totals,
He loses his social standing.

—Jonas P. Hall

Chapter XXVI

My cousin Susan was first married to an Armenian short order cook. She became automatically unmarried when the sheriff arrested the cook for bigamy.

The cook told Susan he was sorry for having such a poor memory, especially in regard to marriages. He said marriages were things he just couldn't seem to keep straight, even though he never had any trouble with ingredients for goulash and never in his life had he had any trouble remembering the 34 components of the sauce for Braised Beef Beirut.

Susan forgave him. She was tired, anyway, of roasting chunks of lamb on a stick for dinner on the cook's day off.

The cook gave Susan his 1927 Essex for a going away present. There was some debate around town about that. Some folks said that the one who was going away always got the presents, but they quieted down in agreement when Susan stated the harsh facts in this particular case.

"They wouldn't let him keep a car in jail," she said. "I don't think I ever heard of anybody being allowed to keep a car in jail."

That was all academic anyway because Susan didn't have the car very long. She married Andy Parsons and Andy traded the car for a hand-pumped milking machine which he then traded for a dozen roosters and a barrel of molasses. I don't rememnber what he traded those things for but he traded them for something. He was a trader by instinct.

He was such an avid trader that Susan, in her fourth or fifth year of marriage, had to hide the kids in a closet when Andy started looking around the house for boot to close a deal.

I keep forgetting Andy's deals although almost all of them were worth remembering. I remember the final discouraging one that brought on his death and how he booby-trapped his barn, but those are stories long since told.

I remember, too, when he sold the genuine antique tavern table that he made out of the floorboards that he ripped from the attic before he sold the old Poole house on Heartbreak Hill to the hunting club from New Jersey.

The tavern table was well made. Andy turned the joints and pegged them just like the magazine picture showed. After he'd aged it in a manure pile for a month, it was just as antique as the real pieces that mellow in dark parlors.

At about the time he was making that table, Andy gave Deak Trembley a box of mixed nails for the peach preserves that Deak's mother Minnie had in her cellar when she died at the picnic in Bennett Brook Gorge.

Deak said he thought the preserves had been in the cellar for about 10 years and he didn't want to eat them. Andy didn't either but he had an idea about what to do with them. He talked Uncle Oscar into using them as a base for a new beverage. He said they could keep this stuff in the cellar and a touch of it might brighten up some gloomy days.

Oscar made the stuff but then he said he was going to split it 50-50 and Andy could keep his half for any kind of days he wanted to keep it for but Oscar was going to take his half home.

Andy sampled this brew just once. He took a wine glass that

didn't hold more than three ounces and the stuff went down as softly as snow on a newly tilled field but in 10 minutes had Andy feeling that the world was a wonderful place filled with folks who deserved love and gentle treatment or even rewards for being present.

Andy knew he couldn't afford to have feelings like that. He left the peach nectar in the cellar. He figured that some day he'd trade it for something, but he hadn't given the matter any serious thought when he found the customer for his antique table.

The customer was a fussy man. He'd been scouting the area and been told he should see Andy and he did and he saw the table.

He didn't kick about Andy's price. He had one attitude, though, that Andy thought was unfair and objectionable. He wanted a written guarantee of authenticity.

Andy shuffled around the request. He pretended he didn't quite understand. He acted as stupidly as he could but the buyer kept explaining and asking and finally Andy had to agree to write out some kind of paper.

He sat down at the kitchen table. He licked his pencil and tested it on the back of a pad. Then he said, "Susan, I'll bet this man would like just a little of that peach wine in the cellar."

The customer agreed that he probably would. Susan brought him a water tumbler of it. He thought it was delicious. He drank it all while Andy was laboring over words and lines. When the guarantee was finally written and read aloud and revised and read again, the customer's eyes were glassy. That was when Andy made his play.

"I guess that's about what we want it to say, ain't it?" he asked. "Hell, it guarantees everything but the rope you're going to tie it to your car with."

The man read the paper again. "It's fine," he said. "It's just fine."

"In that case," said Andy, "just sign it at the bottom and we'll start to load."

The customer signed. Adrift in a sea of peach nectar, he

guaranteed the authenticity of his purchase. He testified to himself, in writing, that the table was a genuine antique. He agreed to buy it back from himself if its pedigree was challenged. When he drove away, he was smiling.

So was Andy Parsons. Andy said, "If Oscar comes here and wants to trade me a new Cadillac for the rest of that brew, stop me from even considering the deal if you have to hit me over the head."

But Susan had forgotten to put the cover back on the crock. The next day, she found four dead mice floating on top, each with a big smile on its face. She poured the stuff out before Andy had a chance to tell her that the brew was antiseptic and would have done no harm to anyone.

Andy said afterwards that this was the story of his life, that just as his prospects looked beautifully promising, he kept running into blocks set up by someone's twisted ethics.

Actually, that really was what happened to him when he decided to enter politics. He was afraid of a block and he did run into one, although it wasn't the one he was afraid of.

When Clint Reynolds first suggested that Andy run for the state legislature, Andy shook his head.

"I don't know," he said. "I could be almost under the wire in a campaign when some stinker might bring up a rumor about my having sold someone a lame horse or something."

"As long as it was a lie," said Clint. "You wouldn't have to worry about it."

"It would be a lie, all right," said Andy. "I didn't sell the horse. The guy traded me a Maxwell touring car for it. But it's hard to explain things like that. I mean, the car had a cracked block."

But Clint talked to a few voters and they thought Andy might do all right for himself. They said that, after all, the people had sent many stupid finaglers to the legislature and a smart one might be an interesting change. So Andy put out his petitions.

My cousin Susan was delighted. It wasn't the prospect of being a legislator's wife that pleased her. It was that she figured politics might cut down on Andy's trading time and she

PEACH

wouldn't have to stall off so many angry customers who stood at the door with shotguns while Andy hid under the bed.

And, Andy Parsons was a personable man. He could sell some terrible things, so the party politicians thought he might be able to sell the party. When he made a speech, the men in the audience said he had sharp wits. Their wives were enthusiastic about Andy's tousled hair. They said he spoke poetically, which was probably true because he got his phrases from the Oxford Dictionary of Quotations that he'd conned a salesman into swapping for two re-cut tires.

It began to look as though Andy might get the party nomination and if he got that then his election chances were better than even.

All candidates in our district, though, needed some support from Ben Thomas. He had a tight hold on the Burnt Creek and Big Brook vote. He wasn't a political boss, but he was the nearest thing to it that our area had.

Old Ben didn't get his power because he had money or because he promised favors or because he had won glory as a soldier or an adventurer. He was just Ben Thomas. Folks trusted him. He had the kind of dignity that impresses rough people and he was completely honest in all his dealings.

Ben Thomas would not only have walked miles to return an unwitting overcharge to a store customer, as Abe Lincoln did. Thomas would have paid the man interest for the few hours the money had been kept. He was the kind of man who returns borrowed books.

So, there came a time when it was necessary that Andy Parsons make a call on old Ben Thomas. He did that. He introduced himself and he stated the reason for his call.

"I ain't interested in the salary, Mr. Thomas," said Andy. "I want to go to Augusta so I can serve my people. Seems to me there comes a time when service must take precedence over self."

"Carlyle," said Ben.

"No. Parsons is the name. Andy Parsons."

"I was referring to the source of your fine phrase. Now, I've heard a few things about you, Mr. Parsons . . . ."

"Call me Andy."

"I've heard some things about you, Mr. Parsons, that impress me with your ability and your versatility. But there are other things that don't . . . well, that don't . . ."

"Lies," said Andy.

"Which ones?"

"All the other things. Besides, Mr. Thomas, you can never plan the future by the past."

"Burke," said Old Ben. "Edmund Burke. Your literary thefts are chosen well. Now, about support from me . . . will you make me a promise that you won't ever use your position to add to your own finances or feather your nest in some way?"

Andy Parsons thought for a minute. He was wrestling with his conscience. Most rascals would simply have agreed and then let the future take care of itself. Some quirk in Andy's character made him reluctant to be less of a gentleman than old Ben Thomas. He decided to make a different appeal.

"Mr. Thomas," he said, "suppose I went around making promises to everybody to get votes. Suppose I promised things to the timber interests and the W.C.T.U. and the construction men. Would you approve of that?"

"Certainly not."

"But still you want me to promise you something."

"Only to be honest, that's all."

Andy shook his head. "The principle is the same," he said. "Any kind of a promise restricts a man's service."

"Sam Johnson, I think," said Ben Thomas. "But I'm not sure I would have supported him, either. Good day, Mr. Parsons."

The eighth grade girls surrounded Alice Wend,
Pointing their fingers,
Saying, "Alice is in love,
Alice is in love,
Alice loves Ned Trembley."

Red faced, Alice shouted protest.
Saying, "I do not, I think he's awful;
I think all boys are awful."

Alone, behind the maple tree,
Ned Trembley heard the voices,
Remembering that the afternoon before,
Shy Alice had approached him, saying,
"If you want me to, I'll be your girl."

—Jonas P. Hall

Chapter XXVII

We were so very innocent when we were young. I am not sure that this was the influence of rurality and I question the assumption that we lived in an innocent age. Scott Fitzgerald didn't think so but, admittedly, Fitzgerald's idea of innocence was far different from that of today, and he was talking about college years anyway.

Some wit has suggested that if Booth Tarkington had written "Seventeen" today, he would have had to call it "Twelve." Possibly he should have called it "Fifteen" when he wrote it. He may have been innocent, too.

In Cedar River, at seventeen we were on the edge of maturing. At seventeen, Ben Rogers was in the midst of a passionate love affair which was to haunt him for years and end in a tragedy that jolted our town. At seventeen, Florence Coosterman, despite her repulsive need to excel all males in everything, was fighting off passes from goons like Elias Kass.

From twelve to fifteen, however, we were taking only cautious steps toward the glory we sensed. Our advances were tentative. Our retreats were hurried. We were impressed but we were also afraid. We knew that if we showed interest there might be a smile but there might also be scorn and there might be giggles from huddles of girls in the schoolyard and amused glances in our direction.

Only occasionally did we dedicate ourselves openly and then we were not sure what it was we were dedicating ourselves to.

The girls were far more mature than were we but that was to be expected I suppose, women being demonstrably more intelligent than men, as Eve proved when she realized she had to get Adam out of that garden before he became a confirmed welfare case.

When I was twelve, I was sure that I had been many times in love but I was resigned to the fact that I lacked the ability to sustain interest. In some way, I always offended. The only comfort in this was that my blundering and my puzzlement were shared. All my classmates understood their inadequacies.

It was that understanding that made us reluctant to accept the mass invitation from the Cranston Eighth Grade Sunshine Club to be guests at a spring sociable. Unfortunately for chances to ignore the invitations, they were sent directly to our homes.

"Of course you'll go," said my mother. "It will be good for you. It will let you see how young gentlemen behave."

I was not enthusiastic. I wasn't much interested in studying the actions of young gentlemen with a view to emulating them. I didn't know how much future there would be in it.

"But they don't square dance at those sociables," I said. "They do waltz steps and stuff. I don't know how. Neither does Tom Rogers or Bobby Trembley. We'll just stand there and look stupid."

"Ballroom dancing," said my mother," is just walking to music. You move your feet in rhythm and pretty soon you'll be doing the steps. The girls will show you. It's easy and it's a needed social accomplishment."

My father was less optimistic. "Keep your feet flat on the

floor," he said. "Never mind trying anything fancy. Slide your feet. If you lift them up, some girl's toe will be under them when you put them down. She'll scream and slap you silly and then the chaperones will blame you for something else and you'll get tossed out on your ear."

"Blame me for what else?"

"Never mind," he said. "Just don't lift your feet."

That was the extent of my instruction. Tom Rogers didn't even get that much, so I shared with him as we entered the hall.

"It sure doesn't sound like much fun," he said. "Just sliding your feet around and hoping they don't hit something."

"I guess it isn't supposed to be fun," I told him. "It's supposed to be educational."

The members of the Cranston Eighth Grade Sunshine Club looked at the Cedar River delegation apprehensively as the music started.

"Now, don't be bashful, boys," said one of the chaperones. "You're our guests and we want you to have a good time."

We edged toward the huddle of girls. I reached for what looked like the least apprehensive one. She hesitated, tried to smile, then started to back away. Tom Rogers ran in and grabbed her.

"You want this one?" he asked me. "Go ahead. I can catch another."

That was when he got it, without lifting his feet, without starting to dance at all. The girl screamed. But then she went further than my father had predicted. She slapped Tom and kicked him in the shins.

"Let her go," I said. "Let's get another one. This one's crazy."

Tom relaxed his grip. "What's the matter?" he asked her. "You asked us to come here to dance, didn't you?"

She said something that didn't seem to have any bearing on the subject. She said, "I'll bet you always win the greased pig chases, don't you? And do you give the prize to the worthy poor?"

Someone's mother was beside us at that point. "What's the matter?" she asked. "Are we having some little problems?"

The girl pointed at Tom. "I was dancing with him," she said, "and then this clumsy boy tried to butt in on us and wouldn't go away."

The mother took my arm and led me toward the sidelines. "You go over and have some punch," she said. "You have to learn to take your turn."

I didn't try for another turn. I drank a lot of punch instead. Tom and that girl shuffled around for two hours. Then the chaperones told us it was time to go home.

"Well," said my father. "Did you get into any trouble?"

"No." I said.

"Did you meet some nice girls?"

"No. One of them slapped Tom Rogers to let him know she liked him. Kicked him, too. Then they danced together all night."

"Did you dance?"

"No. It didn't look like fun enough to be slapped for."

"Pain," said my father, "is a normal preliminary to success. Girls learn that earlier than boys do."

He might have added that they found out other things earlier, too. But I suppose he knew I'd find that out for myself. Gradually I did, but it was a puzzling process.

Perhaps parents in rurality thought it was better for youngsters to work their own way through puzzlement than to be given biological facts with all the mystery removed. I know I got no family help at all when a girl to whom I was attracted presented me with a puzzle that following summer.

She was a girl that I still remember, although I knew her for less than a month. She was from Connecticut. Her father was a geologist, studying watersheds or something in which I was not the least bit interested. But I was interested in her.

She was sparkling. She was willowy. She was beautiful. She was friendly enough to let me walk her home one day when I met her at the store. That gave me courage.

As I left her, I said, "I'll take you to the Fourth of July picnic. It'll be at the river grove. Would you like that?"

"All right," she said. Then she smiled, and added, "But don't think I'm going to take any afternoon walks in the woods."

I honestly didn't know what in the world she was talking about. Why should I want to take any walks in the woods on the Fourth of July? There would be races and a ball game and ice cream and watermelon and chicken sandwiches and fireworks. Walk in the woods?

As I walked away, I was concerned about her mental capacity. I wondered if she was a little bit nutty.

That evening, I sat at the supper table and spoke my wonderment aloud.

"This girl with the geologist father," I said, "is strange. She's pretty. She's thirteen years old and I don't think she's ever been to a town picnic like ours and I said I'd take her."

"That was hospitable," said my mother. "We'll be glad to have her eat with us."

"Yeah . . . but you know what she said? She said she'd go to the picnic but she wasn't going to go for a walk in the woods. Why would anyone want to walk in the woods when there's a ball game?"

"Pass the potatoes," said my father.

"Drink your milk," said my mother.

"And tomorrow," said my father, "I want you to clean the barn and do it properly this time. The last time, you left a pile of junk in the back corner."

"But this girl . . ."

"Never mind," said my father. "She was probably just afraid that she'd miss the three-legged race."

The night you pinned gardenias in your hair,
And won the hearts of all the dancing throng,
I was the most admiring suitor there
And years have made my feelings twice as strong.

I promised you that all the world I'd buy
And lay as tribute at your dancing feet.
But youthful plans have ways to go awry
And mine have met with constant sad defeat.

No question but you could have had your choice
Of men who later earned success and fame;
I wonder if at least you heard the voice
Of soft regret for how you played the game.

If so, I hope you realized one vow came true. . .
That all digression strengthened love for you.

—Jonas P. Hall
Written especially for Kerry Turnbaugh

Chapter XXVIII

The movement from the cities and suburbs to rural regions in the 1930s had no relationship to the seeking of country havens by the young philosophers of the early 1970s. The 1930s migrants were not members of a cult that was dedicated to the formation of a post-industrial society. They were refugees.

The fall of 1930 was a period of apprehension. During 1931, the facts were hammered home. Men realized that this period of industrial stagnation was not merely a plateau in the upward curve of economic growth. It was a plunge toward chaos.

In the minds of workers there was no resentment of the past production of consumer goods that had increased to a point where for the first time in this country's history there was food and clothing enough for everyone and even the least skilled factory worker could aspire to the ownership of an automobile.

In the 1930s, the thought of going back to the land was

defensive. It was not an advertised rebellion. In many cases it was looked upon as being temporary, as a means of survival until the broken links in the distribution chain had been patched.

There was one more big difference between the eager "homesteaders" of the 1960s and the reluctant retreaters of the 1930s. The depression era seekers of a scratch-patch barrier against cold and hunger had a far better idea of what rural living involved. They may have lived in the country themselves. If not, they were usually only one generation removed from that living.

They knew better than to romanticize a return to hill farms, horses, hand labor and homespun. They knew that what they could buy with a paycheck was better than what they could get from a potato patch. They were reluctant returners.

Kerry Turnbaugh was one of these men. Kerry knew all about hill country farms. He had been born on one. As a boy he had cursed the meadow boulders as he hand-scythed around them to get the last feeble hay stems. He had worked the dried beans with a flail. He had hilled the corn rows in the July sun.

At seventeen, Kerry had packed a clean shirt and headed for Manchester. That was that, as far as he was concerned. He was mildly amused ten years later, after his father died, when he realized that although he had left the farm, the farm had not left him. Since he was the only child, he inherited the land and a house that barely deserved the title.

That was in 1925. Through the years that followed, Kerry had paid the pittance taxes, more because he didn't quite know what else to do than because he wanted the place.

But in 1931, Kerry Turnbaugh lost his job. The bank took back his city house in September. Its value had dropped below the mortgage balance.

His cash reserve ran out with the old year. He packed his furniture, traded his car for an old truck, and became a Cedar River resident in February.

The farmhouse on the hill was old and cold. He found a few

dead trees, but after that the wood he cut and burned was green. The water from the spring wouldn't flow, seepage having filled the pipe during the long shutoff and frozen from placidity.

There isn't a worse time than February to start a new life in the hill country. Kerry knew that, but he didn't have much choice. He was able to pick up a little work in the woods and in March he got in three weeks steady with the highway department, clearing culverts. So there was food, but that was about all there was. There was food and heat from the green wood.

There was also a leak in the roof and constant trouble with the old truck. There was a completely unsympathetic wife. Happily there were no children to be deprived but since there never had been children, Kerry didn't realize that he was lucky in that respect.

The wife was enough. She gave him a hard time. She wasn't impressed by economic statistics. She knew why the family had lost the city house and been condemned to half-freeze, half-starve, and half-stagnate in a niche that seemed to have been blasted out of the debris of the created world to make a trap for the Turnbaughs.

She knew the reason for all the misery. It was because Kerry was an incompetent, by heritage, by nature, and by desire. She told him so. She told him all day long and all through the evening. She woke him at four o'clock in the morning to tell him.

She was one of the most dedicated husband critics that ever graced this world. She devoted herself to making Kerry realize that he was a no-good bum.

Kerry was a haggard man when March began to fade. But it was then that fate found him a friend. Fate made a curious choice. The friend was the most impractical man in Cedar River.

Had fate chosen to send my uncle Oscar around to spend time with Kerry Turnbaugh, Kerry might have retreated into a misty alcoholic world of his own and stopped caring about anything at all. Happily, Oscar didn't ever need new friends. He hadn't yet succeeded in alienating all of his old ones.

Fate didn't choose Rob Saunders, either. Rob was always looking for half-starved, desperate workers. He could hire them cheaply and he might have convinced Kerry that his only hope for the future was to work sporadically in Rob's mill, turning logs, sweating and freezing on alternate days, bruising toes or fingers according to what slipped.

But fate sent Jonas Hall. Jonas came the first time because he had known Kerry's father and because he liked to be neighborly when he thought anyone would let him be neighborly which too few Cedar River citizens would.

Jonas brought a few of his poems to read aloud. He was surprised and pleased when Kerry seemed to be interested. Jonas ordinarily had a hard time finding audiences for what he considered to be his works of art, his serious poems. The men at the store would let him read blunt criticisms of the pious or the status seekers or the local do-gooders, but they were inclined to be impatient when he veered toward romance or philosophy.

When Kerry sat quietly while Jonas read love poems, Jonas thought he had found someone who appreciated literary skill. So Jonas came again and again. He came three or four times a week.

Actually, the reason that Kerry sat so silently while Jonas read was that Kerry had built a wall around his mind to keep his wife from driving him crazy. He didn't know if Jonas was reading poetry or instructions for assembling washing machines. He didn't care. He did vaguely realize that listening to Jonas was better than listening to comments about burning green wood.

Kerry's wife, though, was happy to have a poet come to call. She was still an attractive woman physically and her confinement in the dullness of that hill farm had not killed her romantic dreams. The more of his love poems that Jonas read, the more did Kerry's wife long for another chance to sweep some solvent man off his feet and be cradled in his arms forever.

The longing couldn't help but add to her discontent. When the warm winds of April brought a restlessness that she didn't even try to control, she told Kerry that she was leaving him.

"All that lovely poetry has brought me back to life," she said. "You're dead, Kerry. There's no beauty or ambition or romance left in you. I want something more than drudgery and mud."

Kerry's protest was only a formality. She scorned it. But she did indicate an interest in his future.

"Stay here and rot," she said.

Kerry didn't try to fight the divorce action when he got the papers in late May. He was working steadily by that time on the Cummings farm. Ralph Cummings had died, leaving his widow with the best place in the valley. She needed a hired man and Kerry proved to be a good one. He worked hard and his judgment was sound.

By late fall, Mrs. Cummings had decided that it would be far better to marry Kerry than to take a chance on losing him. He was willing. She was attractive and pleasant and a great cook.

Jonas Hall was as welcome as anyone else at the wedding. But when he came calling one evening after the couple had settled into their new domesticity, Kerry said he wasn't really interested in Jonas' friendship.

When word of this rudeness got around, Kerry explained it as being only common sense.

"Son-of a gun caused my first wife to run away," Kerry said. "I ain't taking no chances on this one."

The preacher said that sin was everywhere.
"Confess your own," he said.
"Confess, repent, warn of temptations to avoid."

The men leaned forward in their seats.
Old temptation listeners they were,
Keen students of sin,
Eager to know what Satan offered,
Wondering if he had come up
With something fresh and enjoyable.

—Jonas P. Hall

Chapter XXIX

My cousin Paul was no mental phenomenon. A modern social worker might have said that he was backward because he was underprivileged, but a woman worker who said that to his father would have heard harsh words. A man worker would have been the recipient of a punch in the nose.

That point is academic. We had only one social worker in town when I was young and she was considered to be honest but misled. She believed in sexual equality for one thing and that idea was outrageous to both the men and the women.

Even Mrs. Kelly refused the concept of equality. She once belted Cousin Paul into a near coma for not knowing that the phrase "gentle sex" referred to women.

Mrs. Kelly didn't specialize in such inconsistencies, however. She was also capable of fouling up conclusions, an art that used to be widespread but which is generally restricted today to politicians and welfare bureaucrats.

She read us a story one day about an ambitious Chinese

peasant boy who collected a jar full of fireflies in order to have a light to study by at night.

"That proves," she said, "that you should know more than he knew, because you all have nice kerosene lamps."

Mrs. Kelly was a fine woman, a conscientious educator, and a dispenser of truth and nonsense in equal parts. My life would have been much more dull had I never known her. It would also have been less painful but I do not resent that, since a great deal of the pain was acquired in the course of learning to be tolerant of illogical behavior.

Tolerance of illogic may have been the most valuable thing we did learn in the public schools in the first part of this century. It prepared us for insane national financial policies, for modern psychological explanations of anti-social actions, for the arguments of anti-industry Luddites, and for the wild belief that everyone should be rewarded for being born.

In our school, we made up our own explanations for our personal failures or Mrs. Kelly made them up for us. We didn't know that my cousin Paul was two countries behind us in geography because he had an undeveloped visual perception. We blamed it on his inability to concentrate.

We thought that Florence Coosterman exploited us because she was always alert to opportunities that we gave her. We never realized that it was because our breakfasts were unscientifically balanced, that if we had been given two ounces of this and four ounces of that we would have exploited Florence instead.

These things have haunted and helped us ever since. We have defied the constancy of the truth we learned was truth, although there has always been a lurking guilt about the defiance. Even as we learned that there were more things on heaven and earth than were dreamed of in Mrs. Kelly's philosophy, we were reluctant to apply the principles of logic to the positiveness of her platitudes. We were mixed-up kids who became mixed-up adults and so we laugh instead of screaming when preposterous ideas become accepted social creeds.

In vocabulary drills and the multiplication tables, Mrs. Kelly did her best and her best was good. She demanded the memorization of maxims and that might have been fine if she had explained that there were exceptions.

Birds of a feather flock together. That is truth. But the statement stops too soon. It should go on to explain that there may be a bird or two in the flock by accident or because of myopia.

It was simple for Mrs. Kelly to announce, "You can't correct what you have done but you can resolve to do better in the future."

But the resolve may be negated by the failure to correct the capability of repeating the error. It may be the presence of the capability that is the reason for the regret and the capability may remain in spite of resolves. It may be a habit defiant by definition, an affliction that is not a choice but a curse.

"Apology," said Mrs. Kelly, "is good for the soul."

With her it was good for the body as well because a prompt apology for error was likely to soften the blows.

Is the soul helped by apology, though, if there is a withholding of the confession that, under similar circumstances, the act would be repeated?

I can say to my friend, "I am sorry," and I may be forgiven. But would I be forgiven if I said, "I am sorry that I am likely to do this again?"

Mrs. Kelly said that the world's benefactors had all been discontented persons. She said contentment conquers no mountains. As a result, if we woke up in the morning and the world looked good, we knew there must be something wrong with us for not seeing something wrong that we should be working to change.

Most of us still feel that way. We are still the confused recipients of the teachings of what today's seekers of rural solace call "the simple life."

There was nothing simple in that life. It was so complex and so filled with logical proofs that what was wrong was right that the rules themselves could become exceptions.

We had to learn this early in order to stay sane. Had I not learned it, I probably would have run screaming for asylum when my uncle Oscar proved to me that his illegal and sinful activities stimulated the spreading of virtue in our town and may even have made the spreading possible.

He was talking about the success or failure of protracted meetings, those sin-confessing and salvation sessions that enlivened our town at least once a year. He claimed that these revivals would have ended had he not helped perpetuate them.

Uncle Oscar enlightened me on the specifics and needs of sin and repentance when I happened to stumble on one of his temporary factory sites while I was trying to get a mess of trout at Bennett Brook. He had siphoned off the contents of a crock of something and he was capping bottles in a clump of spruces.

He was not annoyed at my presence. He trusted me with simple tasks and he was in need of help.

"I got to get a good stock ahead," he told me. "The men get awful thirsty after two hours of listening to descriptions of the heat of Hell."

He didn't have to explain that. I knew it. It was one more proof that consistency had never been and would never be a characteristic of rural America. Uncle Oscar always did a good business at protracted meeting time.

Men who had just been snatched from damnation by confessing that they had abused their bodies with drink, and then being assured that by repenting they had been saved, were so shocked at the nearness of their escape from damnation that they had to have a few solid slugs immediately to settle their nerves.

The beauty of this seasonal business for Oscar was that the liquor didn't have to be prime stuff. The demand was so great that anything alcoholic could be palmed off at premium prices.

Even a logger released from the winter woods was less avid for alcohol than were July salavation seekers. They would drink home brew in which bibulous cats had drowned, gin made from witch hazel and wintergreen oil, or rum distilled from ensilage drainings.

All this, I had known. What I didn't know before that day beside Bennett Brook was that Oscar had worked out a precariously balanced but possibly provable thesis on his vital place in the salvation scheme.

"Sinners need to repent and be saved," he said, "so everybody ought to help those evangelists. That's what I'm doing."

"You are?"

"Certainly. I'm helping in my own humble way."

"Uncle Oscar," I said, "even my father says that when you go commercial you're giving ammunition to fanatics like Mrs. Carry Nation. He says you're offering temptation."

"Just this once," he said, "your father's wrong. Drink ain't a temptation. It's the effect of drinking that's tempting."

"I don't get the difference."

"Well," he explained, "if men can't get the drink, they can't succumb to temptation, can they? So they can't confess to succumbing. And it's confessing that fills the tent with paying customers, ain't it?"

"But if they didn't sin, they wouldn't need to repent."

"And if they didn't eat, they wouldn't have to buy groceries. Then old Turner would be out of business, right? And if all the people went around naked, the cloth factories would be out of business. You go down the line with all them 'ifs' and you'll have a country that's just a wilderness with everybody wandering around wondering what to do."

That was quite a dose of rural logic for a boy to get organized in his mind. I decided I'd have to think about it. I did look for one more answer.

"So," I said, "you figure the preachers need you to stay in business."

"Sure do," he said. "If it wasn't for me, they wouldn't make enough money in this town to pay for putting up the posters."

"I would have done that, too,
But I never had a real chance."

Two nights in the store
Will let you hear that twenty times.

Would have or could have or might have.
Delusion or delusion or delusion.
Take your choice.

A dozen had the chance with David Morris,
Late, unlamenated David.
Eleven had to live from then knowing
That in being innocent
They proved their self-deceit.

—Jonas P. Hall

Chapter XXX

In the hills of Maine, January dusk settles fast. A woodsman, holding to his working pace, senses in himself the growing fatigue, feels the faint chill of hesitating change, knows that daylight is turning for its rush to the far side of the ridges and that the time has come to head toward a road.

There are few positives in an upriver winter but this is one of them. This is wisdom, past and present. In this, the advice of the oldsters is not challenged, not even by brash men like Dave Morris, a burly guy that Rob Hill distrusted but who was cruising a timber lot with Rob and Ted Regan.

Regan was the boss. It was his job and he had a right to pick his helpers. He said he needed Morris because Morris had worked the lot beyond and knew the corners. It wasn't Rob's place to argue. He figured he was lucky to be the third man. Only Regan would have picked him.

Rob had been away from Cedar River for twelve years, some for the war to end wars, some doing carpentry work near Boston. He never talked much about his reason for coming back. People asked and he gave vague answers. But Regan and he had been to high school together. They'd been friends then and they accepted friendship's renewal.

The lot they were cruising was on the far side of Truax Pond. The lines were confusing, so they hadn't covered as much ground as they'd figured on covering, but that didn't hold the shadows away.

It was Regan who gave the word, while Rob was still checking out a stand of pine.

"Let's get out of here," said Regan. "I never did like to stumble around in the dark. Besides, this side of the flow . . ."

He didn't finish. He didn't have to. They knew what he meant and they weren't interested in talking about it or inviting intrusion by stressing intrusion's chances. It doesn't pay a man to blow the mist from a ledge pocket when he's not sure that nothing has been hidden.

In the twilight ledges, no man knows where everything is all the time. He doesn't even know what there is to be where it might be and there are many things he doesn't want to be anywhere.

So the three men didn't talk. They moved out. They hit for the pond and came out into the clearing just west of a boarded up summer cottage. They were easing into an end-of-the-day stride when Morris shouted, "Look at that camp door."

It had been battered right off its hinges, not jimmied open but smashed as though by an old cannon ball.

That was when the breeze stirred the cedars and shook loose the cover over fear.

Something had been walking the area wildlands since November. Publicly, the reports brought scoffing. Privately, they brought unease.

Reggie Gage and Alf Baker had seen a big bear walking away from a Burnt Creek cutting on its hind legs. Reggie told around town that he'd taken a shot at it, but Alf admitted to friends that Reggie was protecting his pride. Alf said they hadn't shot at all because it was the kind of thing you left alone, hoping it would do the same for you.

Tom Webster had found one of his sheep dead in his upper

pasture. It's head was bashed in. That could have been a bear, except that the hind quarters were cut off with a knife.

People who knew the difference between an owl and a lynx had heard screams in the night and said the screams resembled neither one.

So there was a little background for what Morris and Regan and Rob Hill came across, a background of belief or maybe unbelief but certainly unease.

Regan pointed to a small drift by the cottage steps. "There's the tracks," he said.

He didn't expect an answer. He knew the others could see the tracks as well as he could. He was talking only to prove to himself that he was still real, that the whole thing was real, that something did exist that made tracks like those.

They were deep and big and bulky. They went from the steps to the snow-covered ice and headed across the pond. But even Morris didn't want to follow them. He might say later that he'd wanted to, but he didn't want to at all, not tracks like those, not when it was so close to the sundown stillness that a man could shy at the shadows of moving pines until he got tired of ducking and stood up to one that might not be a shadow at all.

So they moved away, trying not to hurry but keeping their uneasiness until they were well out on the wide frozen swamp that was the Rock River Flow.

"Half a mile to the car," said Regan. "We'll figure out what we ought to do after we get there."

That cut the tension. The comfort of the car would be real. It would be a part of the positive, an engine idling, outside shirts shucked off, warmth from the heater. That would be the place to wonder what was loose in the woods, what had maybe been watching them as they worked, what might be as afraid of them as they were of it.

They relaxed and let fatigue seep in. They put their heads down and plodded, spaced out in a single file, puzzlement partly dulled, range of safety broadened.

But a woodsman can be letting down and heading for home

and he'll still sense anything that's out of place around him. He might take awhile to know what it is but he'll sense it.

It was that feeling that made Rob Hill stop walking and try to focus on the fringe brush at the edge of the woods, three hundred feet away. There was a spruce that was bulkier than it should be, outlined at the wrong angle, double shadowed, too rigid.

"Regan," said Rob.

Regan took another step and then turned.

"The little spruce by the dead fir," said Rob, pointing.

They both stood, looking intently, seeing no movement at all, hearing no sounds except from where Morris was still easing along up ahead.

"What did you see?" asked Regan.

"Don't know. Just . . . something."

Morris noticed the lack of tread behind, looked, called out, "What's going on?"

"Something in the brush there," said Regan.

Then there was a dark outline, definitely in motion, retreating toward the ridge through the spotty cover.

"Damn it," said Morris, "we ought to bring one gun, anyway."

"Gun wouldn't help," said Regan. "You don't have any idea what that thing is."

"I'd shoot it anyway. It sure ain't nothing that's doing anybody any good. Come on, let's get moving before we freeze to the crust."

In the car, smoking and tapping the stashed bottle for one warming drink, they agreed that they should report to somebody.

"We go to Jesse Hill," said Morris. "We can get away from him quickest. The troopers would be asking questions to midnight and I got a little visiting to do."

"With whose wife?" asked Regan.

Rob Hill was drinking. He sputtered, jolted because with Morris that wasn't a joke.

A lot of men will toss out that kind of question if they're in a gang, picking on some guy with a face like a mangled melon and a wife that would club his brains out if he turned sideways to look at a window store dummy.

But this wasn't like that at all. With Morris, the question was hitting at the hub of truth.

Morris was about thirty-five years old, curly haired, rugged as a pasture pine. His wife had packed up and left him three years before and there was no question in anybody's mind that she had grounds for divorce. The only thing people wondered about was which woman in town Morris was playing the hardest.

There were a lot of rumors, but no facts. Morris was cozy. He didn't blow any bugles as he slid through a kitchen door on a dark early morning when a husband was heading for Rumford with eight cords of pulp.

Rob Hill expected Morris to flare up at Regan's question. He didn't. He did something worse. He grinned. "Let's get on the ball," he said, "and stop minding each other's business."

When they got to town, Jesse Hill was just locking the police office to go home to supper. "Why can't these things happen in the morning?" he asked.

But when he resigned himself to the fact that he was going to eat cold stew, he didn't hurry anything. He wanted to know why they'd been where they were and if they'd gone inside the camp and if they'd patched the door. Then he hit the tender spot.

"You see any tracks?" he asked.

"Yeah," said Regan. "There were tracks."

"You didn't try to follow them?"

"Listen," said Morris. "You go in there and follow them. That's what the town pays you for. Why the hell should we plow off toward God knows where, following tracks that looked like something a two-legged elephant would make?"

"They were big?"

"Big enough. Go in there tomorrow and measure them and see how they fit you."

Jesse Hill sighed. "I'll get some men and go in with you in the morning," he said. "Better bring your guns I suppose."

"Happy right we'll bring guns," said Morris. "If I see that thing again, I'm going to blow its goddam head off."

"Easy with that," said Jesse. "It could be somebody playing a joke. It could be some poor stupid idiot hiding out from a five dollar debt."

"Five dollars, five thousand dollars. If a man's sneaking around upsetting everybody, why shouldn't you shoot him?"

Regan stared at Morris. "Sometimes you're not sure you should."

"Go on home," said Jesse Hill. "I'll meet you at the flow at eight o'clock. I don't see any need of shooting anything. With enough guys we can get a circle around whatever's there. If it's a man, we can talk him out. If it's some crazy animal, that's different."

"All right, grandpa," said Morris. "But, don't forget, if it comes at me, I got a right to shoot it. That's the law, ain't it?"

Nobody answered him. Regan and Rob were on their way out the door, not waiting for Morris, not wanting him.

At Rob's house, he spoke. "Morris bugs me," he said.

"Don't worry about him," said Regan. "He's not as tough as he talks. Even with this holdup, we won't be working with him long."

There were twelve men in a group that started across the flow trail in the morning. Regan was leading the line. He found the fresh tracks within fifteen minutes.

"There they are," he said to Jesse Hill. "What made them?"

Jesse shook his head. The tracks were round. If they weren't the size of a bushel basket, they were close to it. There were no separation of pads, no claw marks, no hoof outlines, and they certainly hadn't been made by a boot.

"Those weren't there when you came out last night?" asked Jesse.

"Last night?" said Regan. "Hell, they haven't been there much over ten minutes. The snow's still dropping in from the sides."

"Well, let's follow them. We ought to have a man right on the trail and the rest of us fanned out. You want to take the tracks?"

"Yeah," said Regan.

The woods' growth was fairly open and there was a solid crust under the light powder snow. The men worked along at a good pace. Rob Hill stayed close to Regan, feeling more comfort with him than out somewhere in the wing. The tracks were swinging toward a line of small ledges and Rob was wondering if this thing had gone over them or found a cut. He was hoping that it wouldn't play tag with its hunters in some spruce thicket.

Then there was a yell from the far right. Rob and Regan angled toward the voice and broke out into the clearing where the ledge made a half-circle. Right on top of a grey slant of granite was this shaggy giant. It was human all right, even though it had a hairy mess of features instead of a face and was bulked out with what looked like hides and pieces of blankets.

"Probably got its feet wrapped in old clothes," said Regan. "Must be crazy. Sure doesn't look as though it will lie down and let itself be tied up."

The giant was making a raspy growling noise, not an animal roar but more like a record turning double speed at top volume. Men were bringing their guns up, hammers clicking to full cock. From where Regan and Rob Hill stood, they could see the whole gang. Morris was closest to the ledges. He'd been third from the right and he was almost opposite the figure on the rock. He had his twelve gauge shotgun up to his shoulder.

"He's going to kill it," said Rob. "He's going to shoot it right there."

"No," said Regan. "If he was, he already would have."

Rob looked for Jesse Hill. He was walking toward the cliff line, waving his left arm.

"Come down out of there," he shouted. "We aren't going to hurt you. Come on down."

The big creature kept making that awful noise. It wasn't an answer. It was a challenge. It had anger in it and fear and gurgling insanity.

"Jesse ought to be yelling at Morris," said Rob. "I still think he's going to shoot."

"No," said Regan again. There was a strain in his voice, an intensity that seemed out of place to Rob, even in a situation like that one. "It's hard to shoot a man. It's harder than you think."

To Rob there was no reality to Regan's words. There was not enough positiveness. Something in Rob's mind was trying to break loose and when it did it was so logical in its being that there was no question about Rob's rightness in what he feared. His only question was whether he should do something or stand and watch while the block of time moved forward with him caught in it.

He knew without any doubt that Regan wasn't talking about Morris killing the giant. He was justifying his own delay in killing Morris.

How long after understanding this was the interval before he spoke, he never remembered. It could not have been very long because the scene did not change. Jesse was still trying to force sanity on a man who had none. Morris still held his gun. If anyone else moved, it was with a slowness that could not register.

But Rob did speak. "Don't do it," he said. "Don't shoot him."

Regan looked at him, not puzzled, not pretending, perhaps also in compressed time wondering how Rob knew, deciding that it didn't matter, that the only meaningful question was why Rob was advising against the act.

And Rob didn't know quite why. It had nothing to do with justice or morality or commandments broken. It was guided only by the fact that Regan was his friend and a friend is many things to a man but he is not the man himself.

Rob gave the only answer that he thought might stop the action. "Because he isn't worth it. He isn't worth losing sleep over. Don't do it."

Regan didn't argue. He lowered his gun a bit and then let it sag toward the ground.

That was when the thing acted. Without any break in its clamor, it slid down the slanted rock and headed straight for Morris.

Everyone shouted, but the noise didn't stop the charge.

Morris didn't pull the trigger either. He was pointing his shotgun but he was using only his voice.

"Stop," he yelled. "Get back."

But of course that insane creature wasn't going to stop. It was going to run right over Morris and tear him apart. And Regan had been right. Morris was petrified.

What happened next was what had to happen. When the giant was about twenty feet from Morris, that whole gang shot at once. The thing rocked back, sagged, and went down.

But Morris went down too, face forward in the snow. That didn't bother anyone for a few seconds. The men thought he had fainted. He hadn't. When they got to him, they saw that he had taken someone's soft nosed bullet right through his chest. He had a hole front and back, the one just a tear in his clothing, the other a stomach-churning mess.

There was a chorus aimed at Jesse Hill, everyone but Rob and Regan shouting, "I didn't do it. It wasn't me."

Jesse stood there in the middle of that clamor, shaking his head, trying to figure out what to do, knowing that there wasn't anything worth doing, really, and never would be. Who was going to dig for a bullet that couldn't prove anything but an accident even if it were found?

All that protesting was for nothing.

Jesse looked at Regan. Regan looked back and shook his head. He had nothing to deny. He hadn't fired at all.

Rob didn't say anything either. Regan took his arm and turned him away from the group. Rob could see that he knew. And he had to ask of course. Rob couldn't expect him not to ask.

"Why should you do my regretting for me?" asked Regan.

Rob gave him the answer he had to give. He told Regan the truth. A man doesn't save his friends from one thing just to let them sweat through another.

"Because you had no reason to shoot him. I know where he's been. You had no reason. Does that make you feel better? It makes me feel worse. Because I did. Damn it, I did."

Regan then gave in his turn. He gave Rob silence as they walked back to the road.

I watch them in the playground.
They have a swing,
A slide,
A fence to climb on.
I think they'd rather have a stake,
A gallows,
An iron maiden.
It was good to say they should come unto Him.
But the key words now are "Suffer, Children, Suffer."

I said that to the Reverend Adams.
He said I lacked an understanding of their nature
And their needs.

Do I, or does he.?

—Jonas P. Hall

Chapter XXXI

Florence Coosterman, the female menace to the comfort and unity of our class in the Cedar River school, was so dominant a figure in all of our minds that we found ourselves comparing her with every repulsive character we read about in history or in fiction.

We were sure that Florence would have made a fitting wife for Long John Silver. We knew that if Jack the Ripper had tried any of his tricks on Florence, the corpse in the alley would have been his and Florence would have carried his knife home to mount as a trophy.

Florence would have been quite capable of saying, "Let them eat cake," and had she been around in Mexico in 1500 A.D. the Aztec preisthood would have been a matriarchy.

I remember coming across the phrase "femme fatale" in a novel one night and thinking immediately of Florence. The reference was not accurate but it was understandable.

I didn't know any French, except for a few phrases I had picked up from Bill LaPrairie, a Denniston Company teamster whose language was a lilting melody. No Cedar River boy was stupid enough to ask at home for a translation of LaPrairie terms. So they didn't count in a test of language knowledge.

No one had ever told Mrs. Kelly that French should be taught in fifth grade. She wouldn't have taught it, anyway. Her refusal would not have been inspired by prejudice but by her understanding of the limitations of time in school.

Mrs. Kelly was far too smart to scorn languages in the way that the southern fundamentalist minister did when he said, "Why should I learn Latin? English was good enough for Jesus Christ and it's good enough for me."

Mrs. Kelly's argument would have been that she had a hard enough time hammering sentence structure and paragraphing and general grammar rules into our thick heads. She was only capable of administering a reasonable quota of wallops and that quota was always filled. So French was out of the question. If we wanted to learn how to order fried snails we'd have to do it on our own time.

But we did have vocabulary additions drilled into us, so I had no trouble associating "femme" with feminine, and "fatale" was near enough to "fatal" to give me a definition that sufficed.

The definition fitted Florence Coosterman. She was certainly a woman whose proximity could be fatal. She was a deadly girl, no question.

So, I said to my mother, "I know a femme fatale."

"We don't talk about things like that in this house," she said. "Where did you learn those words?"

I showed her the book and she immediately burned it. That was the kind of trouble you could get into by even *thinking* about Florence Coosterman.

The worst part of Florence's superiority to us all in the realm of scheming was that she could play some horrible trick, go home gloating and happy because of it, then come back the next day and conquer our wariness quickly enough to do something even more horrible. We were her patsies and she knew it and we knew it. That was why she was so startled when Ned Trembley didn't seem to understand one day that the game was over, that he'd lost, and that he should go off to sulk about his stupidity.

What started that whole deal was Florence's inability to work out a daily scheme for getting one of us walloped by the teacher. That was her basic activity. But some of the schemes were complex and took time to prepare, so Florence had a store of purchased pranks to fall back on when the blood thirst was on her but some bit of complete villainy was not quite worked out.

On those days she would come to school with trivial trapping devices such as flowers that snapped at sniffers or rings that squirted ink on boys who bent down to examine them. Most of these gadgets were ingenious idiocies but there was one that accidentally backfired.

It was an imitation book. On the cover was lettered, "The Reason For Strange Human Actions." Florence wasn't crude enough to offer to let anyone see the book. She made a skilled stage show of involuntary clumsiness, exposed the title, and let our curiosity do her work.

She held out long enough to make Ned Trembley give her a trout hook and eight feet of line for the privilege of being allowed to do what she wanted him to do.

The book was a device probably invented by the ancient Chinese but still effective against the innocent. It was hollowed out. Opening the cover released a mouse trap which exploded a giant cap that jolted the opener down to his toenails.

Naturally, Florence had put two caps under the snapper. She was a perfectionist and she believed that if you were going to get a truly satisfactory result, you had to make an extra effort. When Ned opened the book, the jolt numbed his fingers. Florence laughed so uncontrollably that she could hardly reach out to snatch the trick book back.

But Ned didn't let go. Stubborn or still curious, possibly not realizing that he'd already had his fishing gear's worth, he waited until the smoke cleared and then he read the printing on the inside of the cover.

In big letters was the word, "SHOCK."

To the rest of us, the printing seemed unnecessary, but to Ned it seemed invalid or incomplete. He felt that he had paid for information on human strangeness and he hadn't received it. So he shouted loudly in protest.

Florence shouted back, but we could all see that she was confused. Anger at the explosion she had expected, but not anger at the withheld education. "It's a joke," she yelled. "Don't be such a meathead."

By then, Mrs. Kelly had appeared at the school door. She charged at us, smacked the first few within reach, ended recess early and herded us inside. Once there, she got the details of the fuss.

Mrs. Kelly was not a consumer protector. I'm sure that part of her self-assigned educational enrichment involved teaching us to defend ourselves against politicians, bureaucrats, and other con artists with which the world seems doomed to be filled. So she probably would have let the matter drop had not Ned continued to challenge the trick book's explosive answer to what he thought was a legitimate question. Ned really wanted to know the reason for strange actions.

"People act strangely even when they aren't shocked," he said. "Some of them are strange all the time and it would be nice to know why, wouldn't it?"

For a few minutes, Mrs. Kelly looked at us in a way we'd never seen before, a soft and almost sorrowful way, almost as though she were going to reveal for the first time the sadness she felt about turning us loose in so uncertain a world.

"Yes, Ned," she said. "It would be nice to know why."

The schoolroom was completely quiet. Mrs. Kelly seemed capable right then of hugging us all or even apologizing for the errors and inadequacies of the human race, for man's inability to take that last step away from the animal world that would have removed the vestiges of savagery and rancor and selfishness.

Finally, she said, "You're right, Ned. All the strangeness doesn't come from shock."

Florence Coosterman lacked the sensitivity that would have let her understand that she need no longer defend herself, that she had, in effect, been forgiven in the course of a general understanding that she was but a small part of the horde that insisted on putting others down in order that they might climb up.

Florence was determined to defend herself against a non-existing penalty for being Florence.

"Mrs. Kelly," she said, "When people are *shocked* they're completely *unpredictable*."

Mrs. Kelly's sadness disappeared. She walked over and gave Florence a solid slap. Florence broke into tears.

"That wasn't for playing tricks," said Mrs. Kelly. "It was to prove you were wrong. You were shocked and what you did was completely predictable. Now, tonight, when you get home, you will write 100 times, "I, comma, too, comma, can make mistakes."

What a glorious finish to a dismal start. For the next two weeks, no one greeted Florence with anything except the words, "You, comma, too, comma, can make mistakes."

Naturally, we never realized that this cruel continuity proved a little something about our own lack of distance from the savagery of the animal world.

I had a friend when I was young
Who to the straight and narrow clung.
He climbed the ladder, rung by rung,
While I relaxed my grip and hung.

He lived a pure and blameless life
While I, with indiscretions rife,
Roared down the primrose path of strife
And took temptation for my wife.

I saw my pious friend today,
In sober suitings laid away.
While I, though battered from the fray,
Live on in ragged bright array.

—Jonas P. Hall

Chapter XXXII

We have always had intruders here. Undoubtedly, we always will. Sometimes, through gradual acceptance of the Ethan Allen phrase that the gods of the hills are not the gods of the valleys below, they blend and join and come to understand that customs have a time proved practicality. Sometimes they solve their problems, and thus ours, by leaving.

If there is neither blending nor departure in a peaceful way, one or the other will be forced through undramatic battle. Jonas Hall attributes the inevitable result of this to the mystic identification of Cedar River with the old implanted lilacs.

The comparison may have more truth than poetry, although Jonas would say that in this case the two are one.

Somehow, no one could ever manage to maintain a formal garden of perennials in Cedar River. Hardy rhododendrons, advertised as being capable of fighting frost to an intense degree, might last two seasons. Hydrangeas died routinely. Rose Mallow lived precariously but never thrived.

To get the fragile arbutus and lady slipper, we had to take to the woods. The same was true of mountain laurel.

Only one thing we had annually in profusion. We had lilacs. We had them all over the place. They graced lawn areas, vacant lots, barnyards, and fence lines.

Lilacs accepted the soil of the hills as the town accepted lilacs. Houses on hill farms could be abandoned and their foundations crumble but the lilacs defended themselves against the ingrowing pines and birches. They drew a circle around themselves and maintained their presence, intent on protecting the beauty they provided for the ghosts of those who planted them with love.

In more tended areas, lilacs may be pruned. They may change their shape through time. But, basically, they intend to endure and they will endure. The same applies to residents of Cedar River.

We were happy with our lilacs. Just as in every man's life there were remembered times of temporary brightness that broke the ordinary routine of work, small contributions, unspectacular endurance, there were such times more regularly with lilacs.

When the lilacs had a year of power in bloom, it was a pleasure to be graced by them. They destroyed ugliness.

If the sun shone brightly and the air was still, on the mornings after light rains, the lilacs pressed their presence into every whisper of air. There was no need to bring bunches of them indoors. The fragrance would have forced its way through clapboards if the windows were shut.

But no one would have closed his windows in lilac time. Even the most practical and least poetic housewife in Cedar River accepted the possibility of filming newly scrubbed window sills with sun-dried plow dust rather than lose the smell of lilacs.

Even my uncle Oscar was impressed by lilacs. He used to stand beside them and breathe their beauty. If their season of blooming had lasted longer, poetry might have fought a winning battle against alcoholic inspiration for control of his destiny.

Because in any location where the air is scented with lilacs, a man needs no other intoxication. Lilacs give love an advantage over all other emotions.

Vicious drives for money or material comforts or power lose their force in a place where glory can be recognized as such a simple thing to attain.

Nobody will ever invent a sedative with half the potency of the air beside a blooming lilac bush. Tranquillity in a tablet cannot compare with breathable beauty that can be traced to roots that have the same strength as the deep foundations of the old values he is trying to preserve.

The people of my Cedar River probably made no conscious connection between lilac wonder and their own ability to stand firm against intrusion, to find some beauty in life or to create it from whatever seemed to be the most promising material.

The connection was there. Lilac blossoms prove that beauty can have strange origins. It does not come from beauty previously bestowed. It is not a pomander, created from sweet smelling things which have been gathered and dried and pressed.

Lilac sweetness comes from decayed vegetation turend to humus and sponsoring new life. It is a conversion of the multiple odored essence of the earth. It comes from seeking and sorting the ingredients of beauty.

What a lilac can do a person can do. Some hill country people did, thereby finding peace.

And there was one blessing for everyone in lilac time in the hills. It erased the sternness of other seasons. A person who walked through its dense fragrance could forget the wind-driven particles of November street dust.

He could forget the March mud which often took a heartbreakingly long time to dry. He could forget the January cold that shriveled smiles. He could forget black flies and hayfield fatigue.

In Cedar River, we didn't have stately old homes with histories of occupancy by great men. We had no planning, no building codes, no organized spruce-up program.

But, for a while every year, we had lilacs enough to soothe the souls of a population ten times our size. We had lilacs enough to intoxicate us and the hill gods too. We had lilac smell surplus.

The surplus wasn't wasted. It brought denser breathing potential. It brought lighter laughter. It brought love and remembrance of love.

Of salable crops now in the hills there are few. The lumber camp markets for potatoes and oats are gone. What hay still grows in Cedar River mulches the pines that will soon destroy it.

But the lilacs, defiant of change, persist.

"If I had your brains . . . .
"If I had your money . . . .
"If I had your good fortune . . . ."

A dozen "ifs," all ending with decision.
They all know what they'd do.
They think they know.

Just as well they dream instead of do.
Doing would mess up their lives.

Old Ernest didn't have to dream.
He had a chance to do.
He did just right, having in some way
Avoided efforts to reform him.

—Jonas P. Hall

Chapter XXXIII

Ernest Thompson never had much money but he managed somehow to take care of his needs. He lived alone in a little shack on the ridge road, minding his own business, working a day here or a day there when someone needed help.

He raised a few potatoes and a lot of shell beans. He salted down a pig each fall. When he had cash, he bought eggs and flour and molasses. Every week, he bought a pound of prunes.

"Nothing I enjoy as much as chewing prunes," said Ernest. "Seems as though I was born to chew prunes, to soak them in my mouth for awhile and then work around the outside with my teeth while I hold the stone with my tongue. Don't have to touch the stone with my hands at all. I can scrape around and get all them tendrils and when I spit it out it's just as clean as a bone that a hound dog has worked over for a month."

After Ernest had described his prune-eating process for the 150th time in the store and then set off up toward the ridge with his purchases, Francis Gage said, "Seems as though there ought to be something else in all dammit that a man could brag on besides being a prune pit cleaner."

"Better," said Doc Yates, "than being the fastest man in town to wear out the seat in a pair of pants."

Francis shrugged. He hadn't wanted to attack Ernest, not really. He like Ernest. Everyone in town did. Ernest didn't represent competition. No woman ever held Ernest up to her husband as being someone whose labor or thrift or cleanliness should be imitated. Ernest had attained that desirable condition of popularity. He had nothing to be jealous of, except possibly his single state.

When Ernest had a fresh supply of prunes, he would sit up until midnight, chewing away, reading one of his seventeen books by the light of his kerosene lamp.

He had read through his books so often that they were almost worn out. The bindings were cracked and the print was smudged, especially in the places where he had used a prune pit as a marker while he got up to put a stick or two on his fire.

Ernest was a happy man. His only problems were that prunes were expensive and that a can of kerosene didn't last long enough. He might have remained a nonentity in Cedar River if he hadn't been hit by a car.

He wasn't hit hard. He stepped into the road just as a man from Connecticut was pulling in to park by the store. Ernest was only knocked down. He had a couple of bruises but he wasn't hurt.

Doc Yates did have Ernest carried up to the store porch just as a precaution. Doc poked and squeezed routinely to see if anything was broken. Nothing was.

Everybody would have forgotten about the accident except that the Connecticut man reported it to his insurance company. He said his victim had needed medical attention and probably the company should check it out.

The insurance adjuster buzzed right up to Cedar River, called on Ernest, and before Ernest could tell him to forget it he fast-talked Ernest into taking $1,000 for a waiver of claims. For this needless gesture, the company probably gave the adjuster a bonus.

There was immediate town-wide speculation about what on earth Ernest Thompson would do with $1,000. Jealous women upbraided their husbands for not having brains enough to step into the road when such patsies were passing.

"He'll probably build an addition on his house," said Pearl Gage Caruthers. Pearl was desperate to get a new bedroom added, so she could separate the kids. But her husband, Joe, was sure that a couple of Pearl's brothers or nephews or whatever other classification of Gages heard about the extra bedroom first would move in before the kids could transfer their gear from their old closet.

My Aunt Margie had different ideas. "Ernest doesn't need any addition," she said. "Most likely he'll buy himself some fancy clothes."

Aunt Margie was always wishing she could spare some of Uncle Waldron's earnings to dress him better.

But Ernest didn't buy clothes or housing. He bought two big drums of kerosene and six boxes of prunes, wooden boxes, fifty pound boxes. He hired Fishbait Olsen to haul this merchandise to the shack on the ridge. Then Ernest went down to Cranston and came back with a big bundle.

"New books," he said to Deak Trembley as he climbed off the mail stage.

But he didn't really mean new books. He meant new editions. Doc Yates dropped in on Ernest one night on the way down from delivering a baby at the Sims' place. Ernest had his new volumes on the same shelf where he'd kept his old ones. They were in the same order; four by Zane Grey, three by Oliver Curwood, five by Rudyard Kipling, and then Robinson Crusoe, Oliver Twist, The Bible, Ivanhoe, and Pilgrim's Progress.

"My soul, Ernest," said Doc. "Why didn't you get something you hadn't already read forty or fifty times?"

"Didn't want to," said Ernest.

"But there must be three dozen Zane Grey books you haven't read. And you like Zane Grey. Why not buy them?"

KEROS
OLIVER TWIST
IVANHOE
KIPLING
PILGRIM'S PROGRESS
ZANE GREY
ROBINSON CRUSOE
PRUNES
PRUNES

"Be a nuisance," said Ernest. "I'd be rushing through them to see how they turned out. There'd be a lot of new words I'd have to learn, names I'd have to keep straight. With these books, I can take things easy and enjoy my reading. I know I won't be startled by sudden complications."

Doc shrugged. "Well," he said, "it's your library. They're your books. They're not mine. Listen, it's none of my business but what are you going to buy with the rest of that money?"

"Nothing," said Ernest Thompson. "What else do I need? I don't have but about fifty dollars left anyway. I gave the rest to Reverend Adams so he could use it to help the poor."

Once more, from here, look down.
This is the ridge that was supposed to mark
The edge of the cleared land.
Nearest clearing now is Waldron's pasture,
Half a mile away, still retreating,
Pressed by pines.
The settlers fought the woods.
The woods won.

From here, look down.
Look down and sing.
No use to sing ambition, progress, or expansion.
No use to sing of coming glory.
No use to dream and make the hill gods laugh.
They've laughed enough.

Ask only that the night come softly as the era fades.
Sing Peace to Cedar River.

—Jonas P. Hall

Conclusion In Confusion

He eased into town as quietly as a deer slides into a spruce swamp in a snowstorm. He had old Turner in the store open a can of peaches for him and he sat right there and ate them with some crackers Turner threw in on the deal.

"Can a man get work?" he asked.

They were logging at Burnt Creek that year. Turner sent him out to the camp. "They can always use another man," said Turner.

About three days later, old man Caruthers beckoned Turner over to a corner of the store. "That man you sent me," said Caruthers, "is a Wobbly. He's got an I.W.W. card."

"How do you know?"

"Saw it when he showed me his Social Security. I asked him about it and he just laughed."

I wasn't a part of the intended audience for this talk, but I always had big ears. I was about 10 years old then and I suspect my ears were bigger than they are now. My discretion was better, though, so I kept quiet and listened.

"So what are you going to do?" asked Mr. Turner.

"Ain't going to do anything right now. But if he gets up on the table some night and starts denouncing government and bosses and camp owners, I'm going to throw him right out of there on his backside. If he shuts up, he can stay. Works good."

I could hardly wait to go home.

"What's a Wobbly?" I asked my father. "Is that a name of people from some country?"

"No," said my father. "It's International . . . no, Industrial Workers of the World. Who's been telling you about Wobblies?

"There's one working for Mr. Caruthers at Burnt Creek."

"Probably be a great worker. The Wobblies weren't bums. They believed in production. They wanted humming factories that turned out all the things that made life better. But they wanted the benefits shared. They were idealists. They'd start off in a box car with three cans of sardines among six of them to fight the militia in a mine strike."

"Mr. Caruthers thinks this one might make speeches."

"Who does he think would listen? Caruthers is confused by the speed of change. That's all right. He might as well be confused about that as something else."

My father stopped talking and looked at me in a way that I had come to realize was an admission that he was expecting too much understanding. Still, he couldn't help adding one more touch.

"Confusion," he said, "is a positive need in this town. Probably is in all towns like this. If there weren't such a thing as confusion, it would have to be invented. Take away confusion and what would you have left?"

"Are you confused?"

"Certainly, I'm confused. Why else would I be trying to help you understand something I don't understand myself?"

He laughed. He said, "That's enough education for today. Fill the woodbox."

That was all so long ago that I don't even want to think about how long ago it was. It was far away ago. It was a flash card that faded. The print did not become clear again until I talked with Jonas Hall about the problems of accurately portraying a town that casual visitors thought could be portrayed with no trouble at all.

That was when Jonas spoke of the need for segmentation and the conflict between romance and truth. He mentioned confusion then, not only in the town but in the minds of the observers.

Jonas had only scorn for pastoral poets who found only a laudable nobility in the souls of those who had nature for a teacher and supposedly developed honesty, reverence, tolerance and clarity of vision.

"They miss stubborness," said Jonas. "They miss the rudeness that can come from fatigue. They overlook confusion, yet it's confusion that saves this town and always did."

"My father said that," I told him.

"He would. You make a list of all the people you ever knew here who were not confused and you'll have the membership roll of a club with the admission requirement of being repulsive."

"Which ones weren't confused, Jonas?"

"Do your own research," he told me. "One hint. Start with the righteous who knew exactly what was sin and what was not and were willing to straighten God out if he seemed to be uncertain."

So, that was all right. I could go on from there. I could accept positiveness as a menace, as a hazard, as a delusion embraced. And Jonas was right in saying that positiveness characterized the righteous.

There were the revivalists, preaching that Eve sinned when she reached for the apple of knowledge and was therefore responsible for Adam's having to earn his bread by the sweat of his brow.

No confusion there. But Mrs. Kelly taught that idleness was a sin, admitting that Adam lolling under the grape vines must therefore have sinned before Eve did. Mrs. Kelly admitted that there was a contradiction between logic and faith. To Jonas, Mrs. Kelly thereby proved her confusion.

"In confusion," said Jonas, "lies the only happiness there is. All happiness is confused. That's why brides cry at weddings."

Confused happiness. Well, there were the church suppers and town picnics which were happy events, although there were few of them in the old days which did not end with the starting of temporary town feuds.

And laughter, the indicator of happiness, was confused. No question about that. Much of it was about misery once shared or accidents in which the victim might have been killed.

Freddie Grouper drowned in a futile search for junk metal at the bottom of a flooded quarry pit. No one laughed about that. But everyone laughed when Freddie, fishing on precarious river ice, broke through and was snatched out just in time by a group of volunteers who then gathered, wet and half-frozen, in the back room of the store, celebrating with strong drink.

This episode became even more hilarious when Francis Gage fell off a barrel and broke his arm.

Broken arms were funny. So were bumps on the head. So were falls down flights of stairs. But ax cuts, for some confused reason, were not funny at all.

"You have to remember." said Jonas Hall, "that there was happiness in blundering, too, even when the blundering was a man's own. A solid striver like the hero of 'Excelsior" would have wept at blunders. He was not confused. That's why I didn't like him. He knew his duty and he did it."

"Killed him, too," I said.

"Served him right," said Jonas.

With that verdict, I agreed. Even Bullnose Perkins, who never thought about what might happen until it did happen, would have known enough to accept a maiden's invitation to spend the night in comfort rather than freeze to death trying to get a medal from the Sierra Club.

Bullnose Perkins once tried to lower a two story house to make a kind of bungalow out of it. But the top story was in the best shape so it was that he wanted to save. He decided to build pillars of ice from the second floor joists down to the cellar and then saw out the studs and walls of the first floor.

His theory was that the March melting would slowly let the top floor down to the foundation. But when the sun melted the south side ice first and the house began to tip, Francis Gage suggested building fires on the north side to balance things up.

Solar advocates to the contrary, a huge pine slabwood fire is hotter than a weak late spring sun. The melting was not equalized. The house tilted north, then fell into the fire and burned up.

That was a town joke for years. Bullnose, himself, thought it was hilarious. When the Saturday night jug brought him to the proper demonstrative pitch, he went through a delightful vaudeville routine. He soared as the fire soared, tilted as the house tipped, and collapsed to the floor while his friends applauded.

Bullnose's wife, however, never did see the humor. It had been her house, inherited from an aunt. She'd refused an offer of $2,500 for it after Bullnose had assured her she could get much more after he renovated it.

Confusion. There were and are a hundred such stories, all involving laughter that might have been misplaced but was the only humor available and so was cherished.

None of this laughter implied that life was glorious. It was rather an indication that Cedar River people loved the fact of living.

So did Jonas Hall. In his dark hours of honoring truth, he was likely to condemn all those whose blunders made truth so terrible, but the condemnation was quiet, unlike the condemnation voiced by Doc Yates.

Doc stormed. Doc characterized Cedar River as the final refuge of the insane. He said a man was a damn fool to keep living there and that realization of that fact made him the damnedest fool of all. Still, he did stay.

Jonas never stormed, nor did he ever seem surprised by what he heard or saw, except on those rare occasions when someone acted in the way that writers of books on rurality claimed all persons in small towns acted.

Jonas never expected dry wit, rugged virtue, patient acceptance of adversity, habitual thrift and inherent honesty. He thought the evidencing of those characteristics was somehow deceitful and dangerous. He was afraid some feature story writer would see this defiance of normality and so perpetuate a literary legend based on lies.

"The lies might motivate migration," he said. "In would come multitudes whose gods were not our gods, their goals not ours."

"Do we have goals?"

"Might call them that," said Jonas Hall. "One goal at least. To keep on loving life while knowing that it's mostly pain, fatigue, trouble, worry, and fighting the inevitable. To love life because it's better than the alternative, which is always much too close."